P9-DLO-885

Photography within the Humanities

John Morris

Paul Taylor

Gjon Mili

Robert Frank

Frederick Wiseman

John Szarkowski

W. Eugene Smith

Susan Sontag

Irving Penn

Robert Coles

Photography within the Humanities

Edited by

Eugenia Parry Janis

and

Wendy MacNeil

The Art Department

Jewett Arts Center

Wellesley College

Wellesley, Massachusetts

Published by

Addison House Publishers

Danbury, New Hampshire

1977

During the month of April 1975, the following people spent a day at Wellesley College:

April 7   JOHN MORRIS, former picture editor, N.Y.T. Pictures *New York Times,* News Service

April 9   PAUL SCHUSTER TAYLOR, economist, co-author with Dorothea Lange of *An American Exodus*

April 11   GJON MILI, *Life* magazine photographer

April 14   ROBERT FRANK, photographer, filmmaker

April 15   FREDERICK WISEMAN, documentary filmmaker

April 16   JOHN SZARKOWSKI, director, Department of Photography, Museum of Modern Art, New York

April 18   W. EUGENE SMITH, photo-essayist

April 21   SUSAN SONTAG, critic, filmmaker

April 23   IRVING PENN, fashion/portrait photographer

April 25   ROBERT COLES, author and research psychiatrist, Harvard University

Their visits constituted a series of ten symposia called **Photography within the Humanities** *which inquired into the functions of photography.*

Copyright © 1977 by Wellesley College. Library of Congress Catalogue Card No. 76-051600. ISBN-0-89169-013-1. Type set by Dumar Typesetting, Dayton, Ohio. Printed by Foremost Lithographers, Providence, R.I. Designed by Carl F. Zahn.

To the memory of Walker Evans
November 3, 1903-April 10, 1975

Acknowledgments

The symposia originated in a college art department which has wholeheartedly supported the formal study of the history of photography since 1969 and the teaching of photographic practice since 1973. We wish to thank all our colleagues in the art department at Wellesley for their interest and encouragement. Peter Fergusson was a constant advisor. Ann Gabhart installed the exhibition of 100 photographs chosen by the participants. The task of locating and assembling these images was greatly eased by the efforts of Richard Avedon, Duane Michals, Yoichi Okamoto, Alex Harris, Gjon Mili, Jennifer Ettling of Zipporah Films, Patricia McCabe, Leslie Teicholz, John J. Fletcher of Compix, U.P.I. News Pictures, Robert Sobieszek, International Museum of Photography, Rochester, John Szarkowski, Patricia M. Walker, Department of Photography of the Museum of Modern Art, Therese Heyman, Curator of Photographs, Oakland Museum, Barbara Norfleet, Carpenter Center for the Visual Arts, Davis Pratt, Curator of Photography, Fogg Art Museum, Harvard University, Marge Neikrug, Neikrug Galleries, Inc., Harry Lunn and Maurizia Grosman, Lunn Gallery-Graphics International Ltd., and the Witkin Gallery.

Maria Morris, Hannah B. Bruce, Time-Life Picture Agency, Paul Clifford, Wide World Photos, Inc., Frank Wolfe, Lyndon Baines Johnson Library and Magnum Photos, Inc. helped to make certain additional pictures available for the source book.

For help in the planning stages we would like to thank Kenworth Moffett. For invaluable assistance during the symposia we would also like to thank Carla Mathes Woodward, Peteris Bite, Marjorie A. Dings, Elizabeth P. Richardson, Ruth B. Wilson, Muriel Crampton, William McKenzie Woodward, Rosalyn Gerstein and Carl Sesto. Catharine H. Allen coordinated the whole series. Without her expert organizing skills, it is certain that the events would never have transpired so smoothly.

With Wellesley students it is possible to accomplish practically anything: they participated in all phases of the events, produced the tapes and transcribed them. Thanks are due Sasha Norkin, Jessine Monaghan, Liz de Tuerk, Rebecca Dragiff, Deborah Keith, Linda Mahoney, and especially Lesley Baier and Lillian Hsu who gave generous and untiring assistance in the final stages of the book's production.

Finally, we owe our greatest debt to the speakers and confess selfishly that the whole undertaking was the best way we could think of to know them better.

EPJ and WMacN

Resources for the symposia in 1975, and for the production of the source book in 1976 were awarded in two separate grants by the Northeastern Pooled Common Fund, established by Mr. and Mrs. George de Menil (Lois Pattison, Wellesley College Class of 1960). We gratefully acknowledge the Fund's generous support and the sympathetic interest of its founders at every stage of the project.

Introduction

We are all possessors of a highly sophisticated form of visual literacy, largely influenced by photographs and more recently by television. Strangely enough, an outstanding characteristic of this visual literacy is our lack of consciousness about how it works. We really have not begun to consider how, why or to what extent photographs move us, teach us or force us to make choices and form judgments. Specifically, we do not yet fully understand how the particular physical nature of its picture making system affects the visual appearance of a photograph and thereby alters the information it contains.

Photographs offer a version of reality as subject to critical interpretation as that offered by any other medium. Contrary to the nineteenth century conviction, photographs are not equal to the truth; they bear only partial truths. Photographs "masquerade as 'it-ness,'" to quote an apt formulation. They carry information clothed in a curious visual organization. This visual organization or syntax affects our view of the world enormously. For as members of a photographic community, we are receiving thousands of photographic signals daily. Also, much of what we believe to be true about the past one hundred and thirty-seven years has been inculcated through photographs.

Until recently, many focused inquiries about photography have been devoted to its relation to the arts. Because photographs are pictures with a special formal organization, it has been natural to link their production to art making. A favorite issue, which still has not died, for example, is whether photography can be an art at all. By now general consensus says that photography seems to be capable of artistic expression when it is practiced by artists. Another view holds that the question is beside the point: the history of photography and the accumulation of photographic images since 1839 has demonstrated that photography involved itself in much more than aesthetic claims. It took root in every aspect of life. To begin to understand the medium fully we must examine its role systematically and include it within the study of the humanities.

This was the basic idea behind the creation of the series of symposia called **Photography within the Humanities** held at Wellesley College in the Spring of 1975. While there have been countless conferences on photography which re-examined aesthetic and technical questions, never before had there been an attempt to explore photography's function or its far-reaching effects on our experience—on the way we gather information and the quality of that information. Our primary aim in these symposia was to expand our understanding of photography beyond the realm of the art museum by asking questions about the medium which would promote a recognition of its connection to other related fields, and having done this, would articulate that connection.

The symposia's activities centered around ten individuals who regard photography as a significant part of their work or for whom photography is important enough to engage their critical attention. Our choice of speakers was based on their skill at making, using or thinking about photographic pictures and their ability to speak about it to others. The main objective was to bring about a series of dialogues about photography as a documentary tool by having access to people whose experiences had led them to opinions about the particular kind of success or failure photography has had in its many applications.

Between April 7 and April 25 of 1975, each of the ten participants came to Wellesley College and spent the day. They met with students in informal seminars during the morning and afternoon and gave a public lecture in the evening. Each speaker was asked for a list of ten photographs which would best represent his or her point of view. The 100 photographs, assembled in a major exhibition in the main gallery of the Jewett Arts Center, became a core of images around which discussions might take place. Moreover, they provided the speakers with their only access to the views of the others who had been invited.

It seemed important to have the participants appear one at a time. Although shoptalk between professionals on a panel is entertaining and even instructive, we were not interested in collisions between celebrities on a stage. Instead we calculated another kind of event, of one experienced and opinionated guest appearing after another, each of whom would bring a different attitude toward his or her work. This left the burden of the cross-fertilization of ideas on the students, who, fresh from the visit of one speaker, were soon assaulted by the next. Being in possession of the whole picture (none of the speakers stayed to hear the others) gave the students a sense of equal footing with speakers who might have seemed overwhelming. We could not anticipate the extent to which the ten participants would refer to one another. The same story related by an editor and later by an artist was, in the opinion of the students, embarrassing but illuminating.

Most of the participants simply spoke about what they do when they work and related their thoughts about their work. On the whole, this occurred not in long, reasoned expositions but as little talks about fortuitous encounters; what was said, what was once thought, what changed. These accounts, with no overriding design except that they make up the life of a professional, were undeniably the most memorable and possibly the most valuable parts of the meetings. A striking number of new details about photographic experiences emerged which altered profoundly the standard information about many well-known photographs and photographic careers.

Similarly, as with all direct confrontations with people known only from afar by reputation, many popular notions about them were corrected. In the course of a day, it was possible to concentrate on one life and one career, to understand a reputation by seeing how it had developed depending on circumstances and personal choices. Well-respected models of photographic achievement were seen in an entirely new light. For the first time, it seemed possible to understand what Dorothea Lange's and Paul Taylor's *An American Exodus,* produced forty years ago, meant then, and what it still might mean today in the context of the estimated millions of photographs documenting America made since. In the same way, W. Eugene Smith's classic *Life* magazine stories were reviewed in relation to the recently published *Minamata.* It became clear that Smith's career had a completely comprehensible evolution.

Throughout the sessions, certain names seemed to surface more than others. Dorothea Lange, Walker Evans and Diane Arbus were discussed by nearly every speaker. Every speaker had a different approach to the issue of meaning in a photograph. The achievements of some photographers such as Walker Evans, Smith or Lange were held up as rebuttals to Sontag's moral criticism against photographic practice in America as a process of appropriating reality (picture taking), rather than one of creatively generating new realities with a camera (picture making).

The ordering of the speakers was based on preconceived ideas of what might transpire. We hoped Robert Coles would apply the admirable plain-spoken perception of social problems, so lucidly expressed in his books, to the questions which had accumulated during the symposia. We hoped that as the last speaker, he would, in essence, pick up the pieces. We were not prepared for his refusal to be locked into the role we had expected him to play.

Few of the speakers, in fact, addressed themselves directly to the theme of the symposia. Each appeared as a self-defined primary informer, already involved with the problem of photography's role as part of his or her life's work. Ultimately, in spite of our great ambition that the symposia provide the answers to the most penetrating questions which might be asked about the medium, it was discovered that we are still only at the early stages of our inquiry, the assembling of the primary data.

Nearly everything which was said was taped in order to secure a record of the events. The tapes were transcribed fully and the ample manuscript is available for consultation in the Art Library of Jewett. It was our intention to edit the transcript and publish it as a source book for others to refer to in the future.

Editing the Transcript

The animated spirit of the exchange between the participants and their audiences rests in the spontaneous rhythm and intonation of speech. Translating these encounters into print (automatically accomplished by typing the contents of the tapes) risks the loss of this spirit. The transcript needs no editing for the force of its energy to be appreciated. What it lacks is coherence. Valuable ideas are buried in repetitions, idiosyncracies of expression, interruptions, losses of trains of thought and a thousand other obstacles that occur when people, newly introduced, try to communicate about matters of importance. We are culturally conditioned to adjust to these difficulties. When turned into print on a page, the spoken words acquire the suspicious status of pseudo-literature.

As soon as we had the transcript in our hands, we realized why other taped conferences and symposia had not been turned so readily into edited source books. The events which in reality had proceeded with a certain inner logic and momentum looked chaotic. We were faced with the task of rediscovering and reconstructing what we knew had been valuable.

In the Spring of 1976, we led a seminar of thirteen students to edit the transcript. The students were: Cathy S. Neuren (John Morris), Adrienne Schach Mitchell (Paul Taylor), Katherine Kent (Gjon Mili), Judith Hirschkowitz (Robert Frank), Michele Collias and Marguerite Verani (Frederick Wiseman), Nancy Osher and Lesley Baier (John Szarkowski), Marianne Duffy (W. Eugene Smith), Barbara Clark and Anne Fougeron (Susan Sontag), Kelley Nilson (Irving Penn) and Susan Blumberg and Victoria Furber (Robert Coles).

The editing sessions raised fundamental questions about the relationship between real events and their translation into another medium—a basic problem in the study of photography itself. The seminar turned out to be about language and interpretation. How much of the sense of the original is lost if the order of a spoken text is altered? Often with a new ordering, it was discovered that the ideas flowed better and had greater dramatic force. The result, though more coherent and in a sense more accurately representing the speaker, often strayed from the original structure of the words on tape. Moral problems arose concerning authenticity and the use of fictive modes to reconstruct the truth.

There was the added danger of trying to make over the speakers, to have them correspond to an ideal of what editors, photo-journalists or critics should say, by leaving out sentences or expressions which did not fit the preconceived mold. Ultimately the authority to accept or reject a final editing was the speaker's; every published extract appears in this source book with the speaker's approval.

The illustrations deserve some mention. Many have been reproduced frequently and are generally well-known in America. They were recalled repeatedly during the symposia. It was discovered that certain photographs are regarded as crucial in forming a pictorial tradition in contemporary American photography. The continual citation of these well-known images led to a re-examination of their significance. It is in this spirit that we continue to reproduce them. This is not primarily a picture book but a book of texts whose contents are the principal attraction. For this reason all the images reproduced follow the demands of the texts and amplify them. Considering that hundreds of camera-carrying photographers attended the events, it was striking how few pictures were made. Even after strenuous efforts to secure photographs of the symposia, very few have surfaced. We thank Larry Edwards, Donald Dietz, Stephen Frank and Linda Mahoney for allowing us to use their pictures.

In our opinion, the value of the events which took place at Wellesley lies in the expansion of what is considered to be general photographic knowledge. For example, the familiar American icon, *Migrant Mother* by Dorothea Lange, was shown to have been altered to suit widely differing purposes: commemorating the Spanish terror of 1938; illustrating the cover of a South American magazine, *Bohemia Venezolana,* and providing the design for a drawing in a Black Panthers newspaper. Classic Walker Evans photographs compared to those by Robert Frank call attention to the lineage in American documentary photography which they share. Thus, rather than introducing previously undiscovered images, the dialogues reaffirmed the far-reaching significance of what is already acknowledged as important. It is in this sense that the content of the discussions during the symposia may be characterized as academic.

For readers who still vividly remember the real events themselves, we hope that these edited extracts accurately preserve the individuality of each speaker and the vitality of the original context. The book offered here, however, has its own inner logic and life. Its vitality bears little resemblance to the flavor and flow of the real events from which it sprang. It is its own event. The printed texts are the residue of speakers whose auras remain mysteriously intact. This sense of aura is asserted so forcibly throughout the pages that follow, that the source book is at the same time a collection of self-portraits. The texts implicitly comment upon and criticize one another and as a whole make it overwhelmingly apparent that to discuss photographic activity is to become involved with urgent questions of man's moral existence—his desire for knowledge, his need for sacrament.

July 4, 1976   EUGENIA PARRY JANIS and WENDY MacNEIL

John Morris

John Godfrey Morris was born December 7, 1916, and raised in Chicago. After receiving his Bachelor's degree from the University of Chicago in 1937, he worked briefly for *Time*. Soon, he moved to the *Life* magazine staff, where his picture editing experience grew through his handling of World War II picture coverage. After the war, Morris became Picture Editor of the *Ladies' Home Journal*. In 1953, he became Executive Editor of Magnum Photos, and in 1961 he developed the Magnum News Service. In 1962, he opened his own "picture workshop," the Independent Picture Service. He joined *The Washington Post* in 1964, and later, at *The New York Times*, he served as Picture Editor. In 1973, he became Editor of NYT Pictures, *The Times'* photo service. Now retired from *The Times*, Morris lives in Manhattan and plans to write several books based on his experiences.

I was never a photographer. I got into picture editing in college, when I edited a monthly magazine, and there were some very good student photographers. I got interested in pictures and my great ambition was to join Time-Life. I joined Time-Life as an office boy, and I never got any higher with *Time*. It was at *Life* that I worked my way up the ladder. Writing is so much work for me that it doesn't bother me to suppress my writing instincts in order to edit pictures. And I enjoy working with photographers, who are really like children.

I had applied to *The New York Times* for a job in 1946. I was hired in 1967. I was among the skeptics who didn't think they were serious about pictures. Clifton Daniel, who hired me, asked me what I thought of the way *The New York Times* used pictures. I told him I thought it stank. He said, "I agree with you, and that's why I'd like you to go to work."

The Times doesn't have a really large photographic staff, and part of the reason for that is that in their formative years—I hope they still are—*The Times* was a heavy, dull-looking newspaper. I don't think it ever was dull, but it *looked* dull. When I became Picture Editor of *The Times* in 1967, my friends would make cracks like, "Well, Picture Editor of *The Times*? Do they have one?" Somebody said that becoming the Picture Editor of *The New York Times* was like becoming recreation director of Forest Lawn.

One of the problems for the Picture Editor of *The Times* is that it's very hard to achieve the delicate intellectual balance between pictures and ideas. So often the top story of the day just defies illustration. This is really one of the most critical problems in journalism. Television really doesn't solve it either. You could make a good case that television is not a visual medium because so much of television is just somebody sitting and talking to the camera. There's getting to be a terrible repetition of news on television. The competition between television stations has been putting tremendous over-emphasis on crime news, because it's the easiest to illustrate. So we're getting an insatiable diet of news that really isn't all that vital for society. *The Times* is trying very hard to stay with the important news. The problem we have, however, is to attract the mass audience of television while maintaining quality.

So few people reach out for quality journalism, and it kind of makes me sick. Admittedly, there can be very serious intellectual reasons for not reading *The New York Times*. I asked a historian with whom I went to school, William Hardy McNeill, what he thought of *The New York Times*, and he said, "John, I don't see it." I couldn't believe it. This was one of the leading historians, and he said, "I just can't get that involved in daily events." Well, I was kind of horrified, and yet I must be fair. He's sort of an American Toynbee. He takes an overview which is so far beyond me. So he can say that and get away with it. And I must confess, I probably suffer from a short view of things, because I think I'm over-involved in daily affairs. The situation doesn't really change that much from day to day, and *The Times* admittedly touches upon a lot more than anybody needs to know. You know our slogan: "You don't have to read it all, but it's nice to know it's all there."

The Times has been and still is very cautious about questions of taste. The only time we use four letter words is when they're uttered by the President of the United States. For example, you may recall a famous picture taken by Malcolm Browne in 1965. It was the picture of the burning monk in Saigon. *The New York Times* did not use that picture for the reason that the editors thought that it was not fit for the breakfast table. The American Society of Newspaper Editors has sort of a monthly newsletter, and they interviewed about a dozen editors around the country as to what they did with that picture. Turner Catledge, *The Times* editor, simply said that it was not fit for the breakfast table. The editor of the Syracuse newspaper said that an editor who wouldn't use that picture wouldn't have run a story on the Crucifixion.

A year after I came to *The Times*, the Eddie Adams picture of a Saigon police chief executing a prisoner came in on the wire just before the afternoon news conference. It was obviously an historic picture, so I mentioned it at the news conference to make sure it would get into the paper, because there were still many word-minded editors in positions of power. But the assistant managing editor was determined to make the picture as small as possible. Fortunately a picture came in the very same day, of an atrocity by the Vietcong to a child, who was being carried in its mother's arms. The two pictures were played together, which gave a feeling of balance.

The Times, unlike almost any other newspaper in the world, attempts to make moral judgments on the news, and to put everything in its proper perspective. And because *The Times*'s front page judgment may have an important effect on national policy, on the stock market, on all kinds of things, this is a very important decision-making process. These are value judgments, if you wish. The question is difficult—how can we communicate a sense of decency among people through photo-journalism?

You know, we talk about our "free world," but we have to put that in quotes because the free press is only as free as we can make it by probing. A lot of people still think *The New York Times* is a Communist newspaper because we published the Pentagon Papers. One of the sad things is that we didn't publish any photographs when we ran them, which I think was a mistake. We were prepared to run photographs on the Pentagon Papers, but it would have cost somewhere between fifty and a hundred thousand dollars for the extra newsprint necessary. As a result, many people never even read the Pentagon Papers. I'm not sure that many more would have read them if there had been pictures, but I think this is one of the reasons to run pictures in newspapers.

The immediacy of the television picture is fantastic, but television just cannot be there quite as often as the still camera, partly because it's more cumbersome. That may be changing though, because ENG, as they call electronic news gathering, is coming in. Earlier, I cited the Eddie Adams picture. The incident was also recorded by a television man. I never happened to see it at the time, but some people did. But damn it, the picture that really had the impact was the Eddie Adams picture, because people could see it not once, but twice. They could hold it up, and look at it. You'd have a hard time finding that TV footage, and even so, you'd see it for a few seconds and then it would be off. The same thing was true of the Nik Ut picture—that's of the little girl who was napalmed—that was also recorded on television film, and it moved some people very much; but it's the Nik Ut picture that has lasted in the memories of people. I really think there's something in the preserved work, and the preserved page. And this is where a sense of art is very important, because this is what galleries are all

Malcolm Browne, *Rev. Quang Duc, a Buddhist monk, burns himself to death in Saigon, Vietnam, before thousands of onlookers to protest the alleged persecution of Buddhists by the Vietnamese government*, 14 June 1963.

Horst Faas, *Twelve year old Vietnamese girl during the battle for Dong Xoai, hobbles to an evacuation helicopter*, 9 December 1965.

Eddie Adams, *South Vietnamese National Police Chief Brig. Gen. Nguyen Ngoc Loan executes a Vietcong officer with a single pistol shot in the head*, Saigon, 1 February 1968.

Nik Ut, *Napalm Victims, South Vietnam*, Associated Press, 8 June 1972.

Esther Bubley, *Peggy Coleman, Housewife, Washington Heights, New York,
from series "How America Lives,"*
Ladies Home Journal, February 1950.

about. They can hold things up to look at over and over, and you can
sit on a bench and study them. But unfortunately, we don't treat the
printed page as a work of design too much. I mean, you don't hear the
word "design" around newspapers very much; you hear "make-up."
And make-up can be deadly.

As an editor, you have a responsibility to the photographer, the
reading public and yourself. Where you have problems is where
things diverge. Ideally, there shouldn't be any conflict among these
responsibilities. But as an editor, I guess you are ultimately responsible to your readers. You're responsible to your collaborators in
terms of trying to be fair to them and to their work, but as an editor
you often have to make some very brutal choices between using this
photograph or that one; and it's helpful to be objective as an editor,
if possible, although it's very difficult. That's one of the reasons that
newspaper editors get callous—they make these decisions so routinely that they get to a point where they almost welcome disaster because it means that tomorrow's newspaper will sell.

I think that aesthetic judgments are extremely important in
photography, too. Aesthetic judgment is ignored too much by working journalists. That's one of the reasons we see atrocious pictures in
newspapers very routinely. There has to be a marriage between art
and journalism, between form and content, and this is the message
that was driven home very much by Cartier-Bresson, with whom I
worked a good deal. I recommend reading his statement about photography which appears in the preface to *The Decisive Moment,* in
which he talks about the decisive moment as the moment when form
and content achieve a kind of happy marriage. It's really a graphic
moment more than a dramatic one. In terms of human perception, I
like to edit for decisive moments. For example, twenty years ago,
when I was Picture Editor of the *Ladies' Home Journal,* we did a
monthly series called "How America Lives." It was a story of a differ-

Esther Bubley, *Contact sheet for the
Coleman family project.*

ent American family each month. Now you know, one family in an apartment house lives a lot like another one in many basic respects, especially with Kelvinators and things. So it really took a lot of human perception to make one story stand out from another. I used to try to get photographers who had a rapport with a certain kind of family. Esther Bubley, who was very good at this, was doing the story of a New York housewife. I was looking at her contact sheets, and she had photographed this woman making a bed. There were a number of frames that were pretty much the same, but all of a sudden there was one frame that was different. The only difference was that instead of looking down at the bed, she raised her eyes. I noticed this, and said to Esther, "What happened?" She said, "That's when the baby cried." So that was the moment, you see, of her tiny crisis. And that's when the picture was transformed into a decisive moment for the housewife. It was just that little eye movement that made a routine situation an interesting one. This kind of editing sensitivity is something that we need to inculcate in a lot of newspaper people, and for that matter, television people.

I have my problems with John Szarkowski regarding that. We had a big fight about his show, "From the Picture Press." I happened to hate that show because I've been working all my life to establish a new kind of image of the press photographer, not as the slam-bang photographer, but as the sensitive photographer. *The New York Daily News* put up the money for the show, but John was determined it wasn't going to be a *Daily News* show. As it turned out, however, most of the pictures chosen were *Daily News* pictures. I didn't pay any attention to what they were picking from *The Times* file, so when the show was about to be hung, John invited me over to see what they had chosen. He left me alone in his office, where they had a mock-up of the show on the walls. I looked around, and three-quarters of the pictures were *Daily News* pictures; there was just a handful of *Times* pictures. I was so upset, not because there were so few *Times* pictures, but because there were any. When I saw the show, I didn't want any part of it. When John came in and said, "What do you think of it?" I said, "Well... can we get out?" He said, "What do you mean?" I said, "Well, John, it's your show, it's not my show, and I'd rather take *The New York Times* out entirely." We had quite a scene, but we're still friends.

Well before working at *The Times*, I had gotten excited about the syndication of stories; and we had started, experimentally, a thing called the Magnum News Service, which really wasn't so much a news service as it was a feature service. We began sending out Magnum stories once a month, but I wasn't content with that, so I decided to take a flyer on my own, and founded the Independent Picture Service, IPS. But for some reason, the stories didn't sell very well. This picture was taken by a Swedish photographer, Lenn Brink. It shows a Vietnamese prisoner being tortured. It's not a very pleasant picture. This story, which came out in 1963, was published almost nowhere in the United States, although it was sent to every major newspaper, because people didn't want to believe that the South Vietnamese employed torture so systematically.

When IPS failed, *The Washington Post* offered me my first newspaper job, which was that of assistant managing editor for graphics, in charge of their photo staff. I really had a ball down there, until they fired me fifteen months later because we got into a big hassle one afternoon. But I really had a marvelous time, and I still love them and they love me. And they trained me for *The New York Times*. At any rate, *The Post* at that time did a lot of color. I'm not terribly happy about color for a lot of reasons, in emotional terms. I remember talking with Dorothea Lange about color once. She was never comfortable with color, either. I don't think she used it more than a very few times in her life. She said, "The problem with color is that it tells you too much; it doesn't leave enough to the imagination." I think there's something in that—it kind of tells you more than you want to know. Whereas black and white is more of a challenge, perhaps, to the imagination, unless you happen to be color-blind.

Anyway, on Inauguration Day in 1965, we had six different color pages. My favorite one is an aerial shot taken the Sunday before Inauguration Day. There had been a light snowfall in Washington. Dick Darcey went up in a helicopter and came as close as he could. There's a security zone around the White House—you can't fly right over it— but he came pretty close. If you know Washington, there's the White House toward the bottom, and the reviewing stand already set up on Pennsylvania Avenue. And then there's the Ellipse and the Monument, and so on. Anyway, when I first showed this to my unsophisticated colleagues at *The Washington Post,* one of them said, "But John, there's no color in it." I said, "Come on, Ben, this is going to look like Wedgwood when it's reproduced." The day after the Inauguration, I came to work and found a piece of Wedgwood china on my desk. There was a note from the deputy managing editor, with whom I had this argument, saying that his wife had opened the paper and exclaimed, "Ben, it's just like Wedgwood!"

I really treated *The Washington Post* as an experimental newspaper. I wish I could have experimented with it more, but *The Post* was a little bit gung-ho in Vietnam in those days. This was not the clash that took me out of that job, because that was not an ideological clash; however, I became increasingly concerned about the American involvement in the war.

My Lai is a case in point, and one which presents a very interesting story in terms of journalistic responsibility. The kid who made these, Ron Haeberle, suppressed them himself for a long time. He used to show them to women's clubs in Shaker Heights, and things like that, but he was afraid of the story, as a lot of people were. I've talked with Peter Arnett, who is one of the most capable correspondents. Peter was the AP bureau chief in Saigon, a really first-rate journalist. He was there at the time of My Lai. When we talked about why the press corps never knew of it at the time, he said, "Well, the problem was that there were just so many different directions you could go, and to the Army this was no big deal, you know." If My Lai was no big deal, there were probably many other things of similar scope, although not necessarily the same number of people were involved. It's sad but true that you can believe the worst of a lot of American behavior in Vietnam. I begin to sound unpatriotic when I talk this way, but I thought it was kind of my patriotic duty to try to make people see it differently. At any rate, that's a long preamble to telling you about the story of the My Lai pictures and *The New York Times.*

Mr. Haeberle finally surfaced after the CBS interview with Calley. He got very bold and went to *The Cleveland Plain Dealer,* trying to make some money. He offered the pictures to *The Cleveland Plain Dealer* for nothing, if they would publish them. They checked them

Dick Darcey, *Aerial View of Washington, Inauguration Day,* 1965. Courtesy of John Morris.

Ron Haeberle, *My Lai Massacre,* 16
March 1968.

out, and they checked out. So *The Cleveland Plain Dealer* ran them,
but big, one day. Then Haeberle had them copyrighted, and flew
to New York with his friend, a journalist named Eszterhas. They
wanted to make $100,000. I didn't mind their making money; I felt
that the pictures were important to be seen. But they got all involved
in a hassle with *Life. Life* magazine wanted the story but they wanted
it on their terms. Then some people, notably *The New York Times,*
offered Haeberle some money for just one photograph. We thought
one was enough, from our standpoint, to document the tragedy. So
we dickered with Haeberle, but he wanted an incredible amount of
money. We said that we'd help him make a lot of money, but we
couldn't pay him a lot of money. *The New York Post* decided that
these pictures really belonged to the taxpayers anyway, because
Haeberle had taken them as a soldier, so they just went ahead and
ran them. Then we got tired of dickering with Haeberle, and we also
ran one without his permission. He's never come around since with
his hat in his hand. We didn't play it sensationally; this is actually
page three of *The New York Times.* It was run very sadly, just as a
document of what everybody was talking about. *Life* followed up the
next week with a color layout, which was their way of doing it.

Another example of journalistic responsibility is George Strock's
picture of Buna Beach, taken in New Guinea for *Life.* I think it is one
of the most tragic pictures of World War II. It was taken in defiance
of censorship. One of the rules of war is that you don't show your own
dead; you don't want to show you're losing, especially to the enemy.
But at the same time, this is an important picture. Strock, I think,
came all the way back to Washington to fight the censors on it, thereby sort of breaking the house rules. It is kind of a landmark picture.
Life had the guts to publish it, and it's sort of the way war is. I once
wrote a piece about war photography called "The Smell of Death."
Unless you have known dead men well enough to smell them—it's the
most God-awful stench you can imagine—you haven't experienced
war.

How can you stop a war? Can you stop it with pictures? The big problem with the Vietnam War is that the picture taking didn't really begin early enough in a serious way. I wrote an article about this for *Harper's* magazine a couple of years ago. It was about the whole responsibility of the press in terms of the picture coverage of the war, particularly the Vietnam War. In it I pointed out that the early stages of the war, and American bombing, which was top secret, were suppressed in terms of picture coverage. We can shed a lot of tears about the orphans now, but the first American serviceman who died in Vietnam was just a paragraph. There was no photograph made of that man.

Now we've had a lot of discussion today, in the seminars, about what one's responsibility is in terms of war picture coverage. God knows, I wish I could give you some answers. I've thought a lot about it, I've suffered a lot, and I've lost a lot of friends in the process, including a number in Vietnam.

I worked with Robert Capa a great deal in World War II. One day in 1954 when we were working together at Magnum, I had lunch with the Picture Editor of *Life,* who asked if Capa would like to cover the war in Indochina, while Howard Sochurek came home. Capa happened to be in Tokyo. I wanted to say no, but I felt I should ask him, so I sent a cable to Capa saying that *Life* wanted him to cover the war.

George Strock, *Maggot Beach near Buna, New Guinea,* 1943.

To my horror he said he'd go, so I telephoned him, trying to shout all the way to Tokyo. I said, "Bob, it's not our war. You don't have to go. Don't go." But he went, and he got killed, and it was just a dreadful, dreadful thing.

We buried Capa in a Quaker cemetery in Westchester County, a little quiet place. The previous Sunday we had a little memorial service for him at the Quaker meeting house. Edward Steichen was sitting next to me and Bob's mother was there, and Cornell, his brother, was there. In the style of the Quaker meeting, anybody could speak who wanted to, and it was a very emotional thing. Then, the body finally came back, and I hate bodies, and I hated this big French army coffin that came all the way from Vietnam. It was a huge ugly thing, and we were putting it in the ground. A photographer came up, a kid, and started taking pictures. One of the members of the family came over to me and said, "Can't you stop that?" I started to go over to the photographer, and said to myself, "My God, what are we doing?" So I couldn't stop him. The photographer turned out to be Dirck Halstead, who is now covering the White House for *Time* magazine. This is when it hits you. This is why to me the combination of human sensitivity and aesthetics are the two governing things. Oddly enough, the intellectual often doesn't appreciate these things. I think that one of the reasons we have so much bad photography and so much bad photojournalism is the lack of sensitivity.

But let me go back a little bit. Let's explore sensitivity in presidential picture coverage, from Franklin Roosevelt to Gerald Ford. Roosevelt had a physical infirmity; therefore, there was an informal rule of censorship in the entire Roosevelt administration. Very few honest, candid pictures of Franklin Roosevelt were taken, partly because he would never be photographed being helped. There are some marvelous pictures of Franklin Roosevelt and his sort of jaunty public personality, but there are really very few behind-the-scenes photographs. Then you've got Harry Truman, who, like Gerald Ford, was a very confident, self-assured man who had nothing to hide. Of all the presidents in modern times, I think Harry Truman was the most loved by press photographers. They enjoyed him very much. Then you get to Eisenhower, who, sort of like Ford, didn't have much to hide and was also fairly relaxed, but a little distant. He wasn't that fond of the press. Truman really had a rapport. He was a politician. But it was during Eisenhower's period that television became an important factor, and Eisenhower was the first president to be televised in any regular way. Then the whole business of photography in the White House became more and more of a circus, with more and more people and equipment involved. In television you have not one man, but a minimum of two. With lights and sound, candid photography became very difficult.

Well, we get through the 1950s, and we get to 1960, and there was a story where the timing was journalistically the best I think I've ever achieved. In the 1960 campaign, Jacqueline Kennedy had been interviewed by Molly Thayer, a journalist who was an informal Washington correspondent for Magnum. Molly had just written a piece about Jackie at a press conference that Jackie liked. Molly showed me this note from Jackie that said, "If Jack gets elected, I'd like to do you a favor." My eyes lit up like green dollars, and the day after the election, I called Molly and said, "O.K., collect." So she called Hyannisport, and was one of the first callers to get through after the election

Cornell Capa, *Jacqueline Kennedy with Baby Carriage, White House Garden,* 1961.

victory was confirmed. And Jackie delivered right on schedule. A Secret Service man came to the house that weekend in Georgetown and delivered all kinds of personal notes and papers and photographs. Molly put a series together which ran four months in the *Ladies' Home Journal.* The first installment appeared on Inauguration Day, which was kind of nice, and we got a great deal of money for it.

John Kennedy, who was very sophisticated about photography, did not have a personal photographer. Kennedy started a policy of inviting photographers like Cornell Capa and others sort of behind the scenes to give a candid feeling. This was very important in humanizing Kennedy, who really didn't need much humanizing anyway. The press really had a great love affair with the Kennedys in many ways. And still does. This was a new dimension in presidential coverage, when you saw the kids under the desk, and Mrs. Kennedy wheeling a baby carriage (which was a famous exclusive that Cornell Capa made), and things like that. Then we came to Lyndon Johnson. Johnson, as Vice-President, had gone to Asia with a USIA photographer named Yoichi Okamoto, a very skilled photographer, a knowledgeable historian, and a good golfer. Johnson decided to bring Okamoto into the White House as his personal photographer, which was the same role that Okamoto had played on the trip to Asia. Okie began shooting a great deal of film which Johnson found very useful politically. Johnson was a little sensitive about it though, as he liked to be photographed only from one side. Still, he actually did give Okamoto freedom to make a simply unparalleled record of the presidency, which isn't really being continued today, I'm sorry to say, although it's a little early to pass that judgment. This Okamoto picture, which illustrates the effectiveness with which Okamoto really got into the inside, happens to be a Six Day War situation from 1967. That's McNamara on the phone, supposedly on the Hot Line. I'm not actually sure that he isn't calling his wife, but the feeling is there. I mean, that is for real. This is where decisions are made. It's kind of the way they're made, and I think it's very important for us taxpayers to try to learn more about this.

Ollie Atkins, *President Nixon's Cabinet receiving gifts from China as the President reports his travels. They received teacups, cans of Chinese green tea and mahogany jewel boxes. From center toward right are: George Shultz, Budget Office; Elliot Richardson, Health, Education and Welfare; Rogers C. B. Morton, Interior; William P. Rogers, State; President Nixon; Melvin R. Laird, Defense; Peter G. Peterson, Commerce and John Volpe, Transportation. Aides are seated against the wall,* 29 February 1972.

Mike Lien, *Agnew Playing Tennis,* **New York Times** (page 1), 20 May 1970.

Yoichi Okamoto, *Robert McNamara on the Telephone,* 8 June 1967.

I have talked with David Kennerly (Ford's personal photographer) about this, and he's very aware of what Okamoto did, which was to be able to photograph the really top level and sometimes secret business of the presidency. Okamoto, who had top secret clearance, could walk in on the President at almost any time, even once into the bedroom in Texas. Okamoto could and did make photographs of National Security Council meetings, meetings in the War Room when they were discussing the Vietnamese crisis, McNamara talking on the Hot Line—all these things. It's really a fabulous record, and a lot of it still hasn't come out. Unfortunately, all of this came to an end with the Nixon administration, which was, except for the tapes, very tight-mouthed.

I'm not trying to make out that Okamoto's work was all sweetness and light, because the press was very uptight about a lot of things Okamoto did. It actually wasn't so much about what he did, as it was that the White House would shovel the pictures out at its own discretion. There is a big problem in America about control of the press. We don't really talk about control, but we talk about influence. Every president likes to have a good press and a good image and perhaps the most image-conscious of all was our late friend, Mr. Nixon. This was the kind of picture he absolutely adored. It was taken the day he met with the Cabinet upon his return from China. It was taken by Ollie Atkins, who succeeded Okamoto as White House photographer, or perhaps by one of his assistants (the White House staff is more than one man, obviously). They're applauding John Connolly on the left, and some other characters you might recognize if you could look closely. It's a different style of presidential picture coverage. I once went into the White House basement to ask Ollie for some pictures, and I said, "Can I see what you shot last month?" They were pictures of birthday cakes, and things like that; I mean, it's quite a different ball game. Occasionally you just have to get your kicks somewhere in the picture business; and that ball actually hit the partner a fraction of a second later. Mike Lien caught this—he was really delighted, and I was delighted that we ran it on page one. That was the kind of thing you had to do to get back at the Nixon White House. Mr. Nixon was uncomfortable with the press, and also the camera, so the most revealing pictures of Nixon are those he didn't plan.

Now we have Dave Kennerly assigned to Ford. Ford saw that one of his great political assets was this feeling of casualness—a man-to-man sort of style. It just fits in very well. I've been following presidential picture coverage for a long time, and I'm somewhat amused by the Ford casualness. One of Ford's greatest attributes is that he *is* natural, he *is* relaxed, and he may not be a great man, but he is a fairly uncomplicated man. He doesn't seem to have anything he really wants to hide in a personal way. Cynics would say, "That's too bad," but in an interesting way, the Fords are humble people.

I guess my story is not really a success story. It's a survival story. The fact that I can stand here and talk to you and feel response, which I think is really wonderful, indicates to me that there's a lot of healthy concern about photojournalism. There are lots of discussions about photography from the standpoint of technique, or perhaps even aesthetics, and actually there's a growing number of discussions about photography and photojournalism in terms of ethics. I welcome raising these kinds of questions openly for discussion. I think it's an area of discussion that is rather rare.

The big problem for us is to find the proper outlets for photojournalism. This is a dreadfully serious problem. We miss the big picture magazines. We particularly miss *Life,* because although politically it was very much to the right, it was a marvelous form of presentation of images. That magazine at one time gave you the feeling that this was where photography was at, for better or for worse. You could see it there; it was everybody's photo market place. So we miss it, we miss it very badly. A lot of fine work is being done today, but it's fragmented in its outlets. It's in *The Maine Times,* and it's in *The Berkshire Eagle,* or whatever. It's in the *Audubon* magazine and *The Smithsonian.* In total perhaps, there are just as many outlets for good photography as there ever were, but they're just all over the map. I'd like to see a new picture magazine. I'll never rest until I see a new weekly picture magazine.

Paul
Schuster
Taylor

Paul Schuster Taylor, professor emeritus of economics at the University of California at Berkeley, is the husband of the late Dorothea Lange. Co-author with her of *An American Exodus,* he is a specialist in agricultural labor problems. From 1927 to 1929, Professor Taylor was the chief investigator of a research project of the Social Science Research Council on Mexican Labor in the United States; in 1935 he was field director of the division of rural rehabilitation of the California Emergency Relief Administration; between 1935 and 1936 he served as regional labor advisor of the United States Resettlement Administration. Professor Taylor was a consulting economist of the Social Security Board between 1936 and 1941, the president of the California Rural Rehabilitation Corporation from 1935 to 1943, and a consulting economist of the Department of the Interior from 1943 to 1952. More recently, in 1970 he was the research director of the California Labor Federation. He is the author of *Sailors Union of the Pacific; Mexican Labor in the United States; A Spanish-Mexican Community Arandas in Jalisco, Mexico; An American-Mexican Frontier; An American Exodus; Slave to Freedom* and *Georgia Plan: 1732-1752.*

Dorothea Lange, *Agitator*, ca. 1934.

Looking into the rearview mirror and speaking for myself, I cannot remember that anyone in my profession oriented me toward the use of visual images. My undergraduate training at the University of Wisconsin was at the hands of unusually able and even innovative professors of economics, history, and sociology, but none of them made use of pictures or suggested it. That I stumbled into gradually, not as a social scientist but as a young human being.

I was born and raised in a small northwest Iowa city. In boyhood I lived and worked through summer and harvest seasons on the family farm of an uncle in southern Wisconsin. After high school I worked three summers as a laborer on a 2000 acre Iowa farm. These experiences gave me familiarity with widely different types of rural society, but they stimulated no urge to record the visual images by camera.

As a child I saw the mounted photographs my parents had had made at a studio, and there was an informal blue print of me sitting in a wicker laundry basket. In high school photographs of students came according to the calendar. When you got to be a junior, you got your picture in the annual; when you got to college, more or less ditto. And that was photography.

Then came World War I and the first camera I personally owned. I do not recall knowing then of the Mathew Brady photographs of the Civil War; certainly I never thought of that as my role in my own war. But about that time a new, convenient instrument came onto the market—a small, vestpocket Kodak, it was called. In it I saw the chance, if I took it with me to France, of recording and bringing home some memorabilia of my military service with the American Expeditionary Forces. My success as a photographer was meager; but a 5 x 7 print still could tell of the horrors of war better than my hand written letters.

After the war, my graduate training was again in the hands of first-rate professionals in the social sciences. Again, so far as I can recall, visual images had no place in my study program.

Then came another step toward change. Not long after the granting of degrees and joining the faculty, I had the opportunity to do field research on the contemporary migration of laborers between Mexico and the United States. This time I bought a postcard-size Eastman Kodak to take into the field. I wanted some kind of a visual record of what I was about to see. In retrospect, I think it likely that I was stimulated by familiarity with Paul Kellogg's *Survey Graphic* magazine, which every month presented contemporary social situations throughout the country, combining text and photographs.

Then again, still before I knew of Dorothea Lange, came technological change to prod me. In Mexico in 1932 I was shown a new kind of camera, one that enabled you to see what you were going to take before you took it. The new Rolleiflex transformed my own relationship to photography. I took more pictures; and with the products found ways of persuading academic publishers to print some of my photographs along with my text.

I have been describing my own slow climb up the ladder towards an appreciation of photographs, and eventually of combining them with words. Dorothea Lange by age seventeen knew that she wanted to photograph unemployed persons. She asked herself the question, "If I am a photographer, why do I photograph only those persons who pay me to do it?" Her answer was to go out onto the streets, camera in hand. That was before we met.

Paul Schuster Taylor, *Dorothea Lange in Texas,* 1934.

Her next steps soon brought us together. An historian university colleague of mine told me that in adjacent Oakland lived a photographer who had a small exhibit room where he showed photographs made outside his studio. I went to see. On that day the photographs he was showing had been made by Dorothea Lange, of whom, of course, I had never heard. What fascinated me especially among her prints was one of a street agitator bellowing into a microphone at the San Francisco Civic Center. It fitted my current need exactly. In collaboration with a colleague at the university, I had just completed and sent to the *Survey Graphic* the draft of an article on San Francisco and the General Strike of 1934. I wanted that photograph to accompany it. The exhibitor, Willard van Dyke put me on the phone with Dorothea Lange; and her photograph became the frontispiece of our article. I think we paid her fifteen dollars for the photograph. That was money in those days.

Another step followed quickly. Van Dyke told me that a few of his photographer friends wanted more opportunity to photograph the unemployed, but were uncertain how to arrange it. I told him of my own study then in progress of self-help cooperatives among the unemployed. One of their projects was operating a sawmill in the California foothills. So one day at my door in Berkeley, Williard van Dyke, Preston Holder, an anthropologist, Mary Jeannette Edwards, Imogen Cunningham, and Dorothea Lange all turned up.

Regarding the difference in Dorothea's and Imogen's approach to photography, if Dorothea saw someone leaning on an axe, she would get him leaning on the axe. Imogen Cunningham would see something she wanted to photograph, prepare herself, and get into position much more slowly. She'd come out with a beautiful result, but it was much more deliberate. Dorothea very seldom used a tripod. Imogen, whether or not she used a tripod, used some kind of a rest for her camera. But each photographer had her own characteristic way of discerning what she wanted to photograph.

I wish I'd brought a speech by the former president of the University of Wisconsin, one of the famed geologists of his day, in which in 1901 he spoke of the importance of what hits the retina of the eye. He emphasized that the image that hits the eye of the untrained geologist, the trained geologist, or the ordinary untrained person is the same; but what they *see* is not the same.

In January of 1935, I was asked to do the research and to recommend a rural rehabilitation program for the New Deal Relief Administration in California. I was asked, "What staff do you need?" I told them I wanted a few people with academic training and, of course, I wanted a secretary to type my letters and reports. Beyond that, I said I'd like a photographer. Well, the first question was, what did I want a photographer for? I was a social scientist, wasn't I? Yes. Well, did a social scientist generally ask for a photographer? No. Why did I want a photographer? Because the people who were going to make the decisions about what to do about my reports were in the cities and wouldn't see the conditions unless a photographer supplied the photographs to accompany the text. Back and forth we went. The director of the division put me on as field director and finally the office manager put Dorothea Lange on the budget as a typist. Nobody had a place in the budget for a photographer in those days.

When I came in with my first project report, Dorothea told me how to do it. I had the properly typed text, which laid out all the conditions, gave what history and background there was, what statistics or estimates I was able to put in, and what I was able to recommend. You've heard of wire spiral binding. Well, that was just new and I'd never heard of it; but she had. So we spiral bound her photographs along with my text. When the members of the California Relief Administration were sitting around a table, my skeptical director of the Division of Rural Rehabilitation tore out four or five of the sheets that had Dorothea's photographs on them and passed them around the table. The Commission voted him $200,000 to set up sanitary camps for migrant laborers. So after that, no question was raised about why I wanted a photographer. It worked. In this way our work together began, and in four years came to fruition in *An American Exodus*.

I was transferred to the Resettlement Administration. You might say Dorothea secured my place. Eventually we were married and went on working very closely as a team under two separate sub-jurisdictions of the Resettlement Administration.

A year later I was transferred to the Social Security Board. Congress, in passing the Social Security law, left farm labor uncovered. In the same legislation, Congress mandated the Social Security Board to study the problems of the farm laborers. To do that, they called me and asked if I would become a consultant to the Social Security Board. As we had pretty close collaboration in the New Deal, the Social Security Board cooperated closely with the Resettlement Administration and Farm Security. So, when summer came around and I was free from my university duties, the Social Security Board sent me, and the Resettlement sent Dorothea, out in the same car to cross the country, back and forth, Georgia to California.

Young Sharecropper on $5 a Month "Furnish"

"Hit's a hard get-by. The land's just fit fer to hold the world together. We think the landlord ought to let the government have this land and build it up, but he's got money and he don't believe in that way. Between Buck Creek and Whitewater Creek nobody can make a living."

Neighbor: "A piece of meat in the house would like to scare these children of mine to death."

Macon County, Georgia, July 16, 1937

Couple, Born in Slavery

"I remember when the Yankees come through, a whole passel of 'em, hollerin', and told the Negroes you're free. But they didn't get nothin' 'cause we had carried the best horses and mules over to the gulley."

Plantation with 28 families abandoned in 1924 after the boll weevil struck.

Greene County, Georgia. July 20, 1937

Dorothea Lange, **An American Exodus,** 1939.

We solved the administrative problems. We were in different departments; but you'd never have known it, we worked so closely together. As we crossed the country, which we did twice across the southern half of the United States, we saw at least two things. One was the diversity of the rural conditions across the country. The machine was the second. We saw the impact of change. Will Alexander, eventually the director of the Farm Security, and a couple of colleagues had put out a beautiful study of the distress on the plantation. We sent him our first photographs from the field. He said, "We hadn't seen the machine before." In a matter of a couple of years, the machine, the tractor, had arrived and we just bumped into it. We saw what a tractor, a four-row planter, and a four-row cultivator could do to dislodge sharecroppers.

An American Exodus, representing a "revolutionary combination of words and pictures," was produced by the close collaboration of a photographer and a social scientist. Neither Dorothea Lange nor I could have produced *An American Exodus* alone. Beyond that, "the revolutionary combination of words and pictures" was enhanced by obtaining informally the collaboration of many of the persons photographed who on the spot spoke to us from their inmost depths.

I drove the car and she did the looking. When she said to stop, I stopped. I let her out of the car, parked it, and usually got out too. What she said was, "I wrap around myself a cloak of invisibility."

IF I COULD GET ME A PIECE OF LAND I'D GO TO DIGGIN IT WITH MY HANDS ★ LOTS OF THINGS ARE GOIN ON NOW THAT DIDN'T USETER DO ★ I COME FROM TEXAS AND DON'T OWE OR OWN A THIN DIME BACK THERE ★ HE'S ALWAYS BEEN A FARMER AND HE CAN'T GET A FARM ★ THAT DROUGHT PUT THE FIXINS TO US ★ WE DRIED OUT THERE THREE YEARS HAND RUNNIN ★ THAT YEAR THE SPRING COME AND FOUND US BLANK ★ HERE'S WHAT I THINK ON IT—THE TRAC- TOR'S AS STRONG AGAINST US AS THE DROUGHT ★ WE MADE A DOLLAR WORKIN FROM DAWN TILL YOU JUST CAN'T SEE ★ THE MONEY MEN GOT THAT COUN- TRY—THEY RUN IT WHAT I MEAN ★ THEM MEN THAT'S DOIN THE TALKIN FOR THE COUNTRY IS THE BIG LANDOWNERS ★ THE FARMALL IS KNOCKING OUR RENTERS OUT OF THEIR PLACES AND SCATTERING THEM ALL OVER ★ THEY DON'T STOP TO SHUT THE DOOR THEY JUST WALK OUT ★ HE CLAIMS TRACTORS IS RIGHT SMART CHEAPER ★ THEY TAKE THE REDUCTION MONEY AND KICK US OFF AND BUY FARMALLS ★ WE CAN WORK THIS LAND AS GOOD AS ANYBODY. WE WAS RAISED ON IT ★ ALL WE GOT TO START WITH IS A FAMILY OF KIDS ★ I HEERED TELL OF THIS HERE IRRIGATION, PLENTY OF WATER AND PLENTY TO EAT ★ SEEMS LIKE PEOPLE HERE IS CRAZY ABOUT CALIFORNIA—THEY GO IN DROVES ★ HE'S GOT THE OREGON iTCH ★ SON TO FATHER: YOU DIDN'T KNOW THE WORLD WAS SO WIDE. FATHER TO SON: NO, BUT I KNEW WHAT I WAS GOIN TO HAVE FOR BREAKFAST ★ THIS IS A HARD LIFE TO SWALLOW BUT I JUST COULDN'T SIT BACK THERE AND LOOK TO SOMEONE TO FEED US ★ LIVIN A BUM'S LIFE SOON MAKES A BUM OUT OF YOU. YOU GET STARTED AND YOU CAN'T STOP ★ MAKIN A LIVIN EVEN THIS KIND OF A LIVIN BEATS STARVIN TO DEATH. BACK THERE WE LIKE TO STARVE TO DEATH ★ NIGH TO NOTHIN AS EVER I SEE ★ BURNED OUT, BLOWED OUT, EAT OUT, TRACTORED OUT ★ YESSIR, WE'RE STARVED STALLED AND STRANDED ★ I WOULDN'T HAVE RELIEF NO WAY IT WAS FIXED ★ IF YOU DON'T HAVE TO GO TO THE GOVERNMENT MAN FOR WHAT BREAD YOU EAT I LIKE IT BETTER ★ LOTS OF EM HARP ABOUT THE WPA RELIEF. BUT THE BIG PLOW-UP CHECK WHAT'S THAT BUT RELIEF? ★ WE AIN'T NO PAUPERS. WE HOLD OURSELVES TO BE WHITE FOLKS. WE DON'T WANT NO RELIEF. BUT WHAT WE DO WANT IS A CHANST TO MAKE AN HONEST LIVING LIKE WHAT WE WAS RAISED ★ SHE SAYS, WHY DIDN'T YOU STAY THERE—WHEN I SAYS I COME FROM TEXAS ★ WHEN YOU GITS DOWN TO YOUR LAST BEAN YOUR BACKBONE AND YOUR NAVEL SHAKES DICE TO SEE WHICH GITS IT ★ YOU EAT IT UP FASTER THAN YOU CAN MAKE IT ★ I HAVEN'T NOTHIN TO GO BACK TO ★ I COULDN'T DO NOTHIN IF I WENT BACK ★ THIS LIFE IS SIMPLICITY BOILED DOWN ★ A PICTURE OF ME CAIN'T DO NO HARM ★ WE TRUST IN THE LORD AND DON'T EXPECT MUCH ★ WE GOT ENOUGH TROUBLES WITHOUT GOING COMMUNIST ★ CHRIST I'LL DIE BEFORE I'LL SAY I'D BRING UP A BUNCH OF KIDS LIVING THIS WAY ★ I'VE WROTE BACK THAT WE'RE WELL AND SUCH AS THAT, BUT I NEVER HAVE WROTE THAT WE LIVE IN A TENT ★ THEY SAY WE TOOK WORK CHEAP BUT YOU'VE GOT TO TAKE WORK CHEAP AND WE DIDN'T WANT NO RELIEF ★ WHEN THEY GET THROUGH WORKING YOU THEY WANT YOU OUT OF THE WAY ★ I WAS BORN AND RAISED A 100 PERCENT AMERICAN. I FOUGHT AND I'M PROUD OF IT THINKIN I WAS HELPIN THE GOVERNMENT AND MY FAMILY ★ WE LIVE MOST ANYWHERE IN GENERAL WHERE THERE'S WORK ★ TAIN'T HARDLY FAIR. THEY HOLLER THAT WE AIN'T CITIZENS BUT THEIR FRUIT WOULD ROT IF WE DIDN'T COME ★ BROTHER, HIT'S PICK SEVENTY-FIVE CENT COTTON OR STARVE. ★ BROTHER, HIT'S PICK SEVENTY-FIVE CENT COTTON OR ELSE ★ MY BOYS ARE AMERICAN CITIZENS. IF WAR WAS DECLARED THEY'D HAVE TO FIGHT NO MATTER WHERE THEY WAS. I DON'T SEE WHY WE CAN'T BE CITIZENS BECAUSE WE MOVE AROUND WITH THE FRUIT TRYIN TO MAKE A LIVIN ★ A HUMAN BEING HAS A RIGHT TO STAND LIKE A TREE HAS A RIGHT TO STAND

Dorothea Lange and Paul Schuster
Taylor. End paper, **An American
Exodus**, 1939.

Dorothea Lange, **An American Exodus,**
1939.

Dorothea Lange, **An American Exodus,**
1939.

Psychologically, that's how she took care of herself. When I got out of the car I think I helped her. We would usually just saunter up to people. Usually I walked a couple of steps ahead of her, let her come up behind with her camera. In those days it was a Rolleiflex, so there it was carried amidships. Usually I would open the conversation. I had to learn how to approach people whom I didn't know and who didn't know me. I learned that the best way to approach someone was to start with a question that would sound natural from a stranger. For example, "Can you tell me how far it is to the next town?" The answer didn't make any difference. When Dorothea was with me, I could pull out my notebook more easily. I think I diverted their attention from Dorothea and attracted it to myself and she was able to start working without raising a question. If, after a while, they raised a question, and they not infrequently did, we would explain that the government had sent us out to talk with the people of the country and get the story of how things looked from their point of view, and then tell it to Washington.

Dorothea was not dependent upon me, however. She could do it herself, as "Migrant Mother" showed us how very well she could. In fact, I've always remembered that I was never around when she took her most famous pictures. But I don't want any inferences drawn from that.

I think being a woman was a great advantage to Dorothea. I think it made approaches to people easier; she stirred up less resistance from people. When she was alone, she'd walk up to them, never aggressive. If she detected any resistance, she folded the camera down, in effect saying, "Oh, I'm not going to photograph you." And I'm sure that, not infrequently, since I saw it sometimes when I was there, having closed it, after a while when the atmosphere changed, she would open it again and she'd get her photograph.

Dorothea used a Rolleiflex a great deal, followed by the Hasselblad, which was similar to the Rolleiflex. Later, she used a 4 x 5 Eastman Kodak and later, 35 mm cameras, a Nikon and Leica, I think. She didn't use a 35 mm camera at first because the quality of the film was not good enough to permit the enlargement she wanted. It was too grainy. As the film improved, she turned more and more to the 35 mm camera.

One of the things Dorothea said to me was that originally she destroyed the negatives that were defective. Later, she changed her method. The trouble was that she found that when the whole negative was defective, there was so often a part of it which apparently had moved her to take the photograph. She would enlarge that particular part and get something akin to what she wanted in the original taking of the photograph. That was something that she learned of her own methods.

I think she did a minimum of talking, the least she had to do. She listened mostly, I'm sure, and it was her attitude, this "cloak of invisibility," which protected her, drew them out, and reassured them. She came away with what *they* said. I remember very little of what she said. The endpapers of *An American Exodus* are words. That's what *they* said. A major part of those were said to her. What she usually did, if I was close by (I had a pocket notebook) was sidle over to me and say what they had said to her down the hill from me. When asked about her ability to do this, I have answered, "In my experience, her ear was as good as her eye."

I don't know when the idea of a book came into our minds. I think it was Dorothea's idea. We had too many children around to work in peace and privacy. This was in the Depression when you could rent an apartment for fifteen dollars. So, about a half a mile from our house, she rented a third floor apartment. The reason she wanted an apartment was so that she could lay the photographs out on the floor and see which should be paired together on opposing pages. Dorothea wanted themes because she believed that photographs can have relationships with each other, and in their relationships tell far more than the isolated prints. That's how the book was prepared. We tied the words and documentation to the photographs.

The book has two impacts. Of course, the large growers in California didn't welcome our program for sanitary camps for migrants. What they wanted was federal money out of the Treasury at a low rate of interest so they could build the camps and have control over them. One day a grower came to my office and wanted to know how big the camps were to be. I said I thought they were to be two hundred families per camp. He said that was too many because the workers were likely to organize. And then so many of the newspapers, apparently from the far left, called me names for proposing camps for migrants which would be run by the growers. And at one of the first of two camps, some people came in with growers' interest who said they were not going to allow any organization; they would come in there if necessary with guns. Now the rest of the impact, which kind of deflates me. We were coming out of the Depression with news of the outbreak of war in Europe and the possibility that we might become involved. People had had enough of the Depression. So, when the publishers made it into a book, it went out of print in no time flat. I bought twelve copies myself at one dollar apiece. So you see, the impact may or may not depend on the merits of the book. The merits of the book may look different to different people at different times. A revised edition of *An American Exodus* published in 1969 is out of print.

One thing that strikes me is the relatively minor participation by historians, political scientists, economists, psychologists, and geologists in photography. Anthropologists appreciate photographs more than the sociologists because the early anthropologists in this country realized that there were only a few Indians left who were tribal in character; and it's now or never. So they took a camera along with them. Besides, the Indians didn't read or write. So, you couldn't rely on that kind of documentation. If you wanted to show what they looked like, dressed like, you had to take a camera along. The anthropologists from then right down to the present time have been perhaps the leaders in the social sciences and humanities in the use of photography. Of course, one of the obstacles, not a conscious obstacle, but the foot dragging, is my own profession. We weren't raised to use visual images for our work in economics. Text, and later on, statistics. But photographs? Well, anthropologists used them perhaps, but hardly anybody else. There was never one person at the top of the field, at the top university, that ever hinted to me that photography would be a good source of documentation.

Photography is a language. So are words. And if you put these two together, thats' fine. The geographer has a language—maps. A geologist uses maps too. And the statistician uses numbers. The specialization of each is not hard to understand; and there can be considerable enrichment by joining as many languages as are relevant.

You see, photography is a language. So are words. And if you put these two together, that's fine. The geographer has a language—it's maps. A geologist uses maps too. And the statistician uses numbers. The specialization of each is not hard to understand; and there can be considerable enrichment by joining as many languages as are relevant.

Dorothea Lange herself gave serious thought to the place of photography within the humanities. Under the title "Documentary Photography" she made this contribution to Ansel Adams' 1940 book *A Pageant of Photography:*

> Documentary photography records the social scene of our time. It mirrors the present and documents the future. Its focus is man in his relation to mankind. It records his customs at work, at war, at play, or his round of activities through twenty-four hours of the day, the cycles of the seasons, or the span of a life. It portrays his institutions—family, church, government, political organizations, social clubs, labor unions. It shows not merely their facades, but seeks to reveal the manner in which they function, absorb the life, hold the loyalty, and influence the behavior of human beings. It is concerned with methods of work and the dependence of workmen on each other and on their employers. It is preeminently suited to build a record of change. Advancing technology raises the standards of living, creates unemployment, changes the faces of cities and of the agricultural landscape. The evidence of these trends—the simultaneous existence of the past, present, and the portent of the future—is conspicuous in old and new forms, old and new customs, on every hand. Documentary photography stands on its own merits and has validity by itself. A single photographic print may be "news," a "portrait," "art," or "documentary"—any of these, all of them, or none. Among the tools of social sciences—graphs, statistics, maps, and text—documentation by photograph now is assuming place. Documentary photography invites and needs participation by amateurs as well as by professionals. Only through the interested work of amateurs who choose themes and follow them can documentation by the camera of our age and our complex society be intimate, pervasive, and adequate.

Dorothea is known for her photographs outside the family. She photographed also within the family. Some people, with their cameras, begin to see when they dash out the front door, away from home. She could see within and around the home as well as she could see outside. Do you know *To A Cabin?* That's where the family gathered under special circumstances. She took pictures of the family and friends on the beach, swimming, in various forms of attire, running up and down the beach; and the dogs running up and down the beach with them. So you had a photograph, a record of the family on the beach of the Pacific Ocean, at play. When the book came out, it was reviewed under the title, "a very different Dorothea Lange." Photographers tend to become labeled by some of their important works so that the vision appears to be limited, in a way, almost as though by horses' blinders.

Dorothea Lange, **To a Cabin,** 1973.

Dorothea Lange, **To a Cabin,** 1973.

Dorothea Lange, *Paul Taylor,* **To a Cabin,** 1973.

Dorothea Lange, **To a Cabin,** 1973.

The land on which those cabins are sited was taken over by the State Park Department. The State purchased it from the landowners. We were simply tenants, along with fifteen or sixteen others. And, for whatever reason, the Park Department decided it wanted to raze those cabins. She showed what she saw, the value of those cabins to her family, by arranging for the publication of the book. Then came her final illness and she couldn't do it. But she left the photographs behind. Margaretta Mitchell, cooperating, produced *To A Cabin* with her own and Dorothea's photographs, separated, not mixed; different, and yet in perfect harmony.

The people of California voted a commission to examine the preservation of the coastline of California. A newspaper man, a friend of mine who didn't know Dorothea, gave the book to the chairman of the coastal commission. The chairman put on his knapsack, so I'm told, and walked down to the cabins. As a result, the coastal commission forbade razing the cabins so long as it had jurisdiction. Which means, well, maybe another year. After that, who knows? But at least they held it up.

Photography doesn't need to be just an avocation. You can have a purpose; you can get something done. I've given one example, where Dorothea's *To A Cabin* is, for the time being at least, attaining a result which was no part of her intention, because when she took the photographs she didn't know that razing the cabins was going to be proposed by anybody. So, taking photographs, you never know when you're doing more than making a record of something. You never know when you're really moving somebody to do something. Of course, the star illustration of moving somebody to do something is "Migrant Mother."

In 1936 the pea crop at Nipomo, California had frozen, and without earnings the migrant pea pickers literally were starving. There was no employment; there was no money; there was no food; there was no relief.

Dorothea had been out in the field in southern California photographing the migrants. When she came up the coast, she passed Nipomo. It was the first place that she had photographed the year before when she became a member of my team for the Rural Rehabilitation Division of the Emergency Relief Administration. I had taken her down there. I didn't know how they would receive a photographer. Here they were, in distress, at the bottom of the social and economic ladder. So I had assigned one of my staff assistants to carry her camera equipment. I told both of them, "I don't care if, on the first day, you don't take a single photograph. I don't want any untoward events to take place. I don't know how the people will receive a photographer." Well, in no time flat, Dorothea had her camera out and was photographing the people. There was not a single incident. A year later, she drove past Nipomo. She got twenty miles north. Then something inside her moved her to return. So, she turned the car around, went back that twenty miles, and went into the original pea camp that she'd known. The result was six negatives, one of them "Migrant Mother."

The migrant mother's distress was written all over her face and the postures of her children. I've asked Dorothea what she said, and this is somewhat unusual. Dorothea did not recall the words of the conversation, but she knew the conditions. They had sold the tires off the car in order to get a few dollars for food.

Dorothea Lange, *Migrant Mother,*
Nipomo, California, 1936.
The Museum of Modern Art.

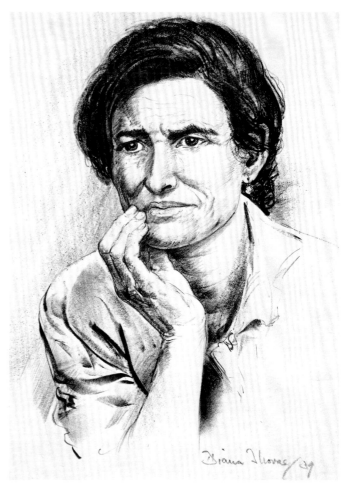

Magazine cover, *Bohemia Venezolana,*
10 May 1964.

Diana Thorne, *Spanish Mother, The
Terror of 1938,* lithograph, 1939.
The Museum of Modern Art.

Malik, *Back Page of Black Panthers'
Newspaper,* 1973. Courtesy of Paul
Taylor.

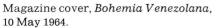

Dorothea took prints over to the *San Francisco News* as soon as she could develop the negatives and make the prints, which took, I suppose, a day or two. The *News* ran an editorial on the starving pea pickers and spoke of the chance visit of a government photographer, unnamed, of course. Nobody named a photographer in those days. The paper produced two photographs, neither one "Migrant Mother," but both of her and her children. It notified the Relief Administration. In no time, food was on the way from southern California to the Nipomo pea pickers.

A good many years later, a woman, through an attorney, raised objections when she saw the spreading use of the photograph of herself. It hurt Dorothea very much. What appears to have taken place is that the woman married a man of some means and, I suppose, didn't like the photograph of her face and her distress spread all over. I don't think she was ever able to collect any money. She never tried further with Dorothea. In fact, I don't think she tried directly with Dorothea, because Dorothea got the word secondhand from a publisher.

What I'm doing is telling you that if you want to move people, photographs surely have the power to do it. I speak as one who uses words most of the time. Sometimes I think I get results; sometimes I think I move people; sometimes I think I don't. Photographs have the power to move people beyond words.

That was the first effect of the pictures. The next effect was to spread reproductions of "Migrant Mother" almost around the world. Dorothea said, "That photograph seems to have a life of its own."

Initially I likened the photograph to a madonna and child in the tradition of Raphael. Now I add that "Migrant Mother" has entered the realm of folklore.

About 1960, the Latin American magazine *Bohemia* reproduced "Migrant Mother" on its cover. In doing so, *Bohemia* took the liberty, first of turning the head of one of the children around to show its face, next of coloring the original black and white photograph, and finally of giving no credit to the photographer. I think it's okay. It shows real approval of the "Migrant Mother." I'm pleased with the observation. It shows how widely the photograph is seen and appreciated.

Confirmation came about two years ago in California. The Black Panthers newspaper reproduced, full page, its own version of what unmistakably had begun as "Migrant Mother." It was hand drawn in black and white, showing frizzy hair and the eyes of a black woman. Once again, the criteria of folklore in song and verse were met in this photograph. Since it belongs to the folk, anyone is at liberty to reproduce it without crediting its original source, to do so with variations as desired, retaining only recognizable essentials of the original. "Migrant Mother" has entered the realm of folklore, along with its other places in the areas of documentation and art.

Gjon
Mili

Gjon Mili was born in Kerce, Southern
Albania, and spent his boyhood in Rumania. He came to America when he
was eighteen in 1923, and received his
B.S. in Electrical Engineering from the
Massachusetts Institute of Technology
in 1927. He was a graduate student with
Westinghouse Electric and Manufac-
turing Co. in 1928, and then a lighting
research engineer with the Westinghouse Lamp Division, from 1928-1938.
He has written numerous technical
papers on his researches in light
projection, optics, and photography. He
developed the biplane filament lamp,
the brightest tungsten light source
then available. He has also done considerable work interpreting photomet-
ric concepts by means of photographs
of beam patterns, filament images, and
lighted glassware. Between 1930 and
1935 he developed the lighting technique now used universally in color
photography with high intensity incan-
descent and photoflash lamps. He has
also been involved since 1938 in experimental and commercial high-speed
flash photography, in cooperation with
Dr. H. E. Edgerton of the Massachusetts
Institute of Technology. Mili's career
as a professional photographer began
when his photographs of the tennis
champion Bobby Riggs in action were
published in *Life Magazine* (September
16, 1938); since then his by-line has appeared constantly in the pages of *Life*.

In the fall of 1969 he gave a series of
lectures at Yale University on "The
Photo Essay;" and he taught at the
Summer Art Project sponsored by
Sarah Lawrence College at La Coste,
France, during 1972, 1973 and 1974. He
is at present an instructor in the "Prin-
ciples of Photography" at Hunter College, New York, where he has taught
since 1973.

Fifty-two years ago when I started learning this business—and I find that I am still learning—photography was a new course at M.I.T. I enrolled in it out of curiosity. My first experiment was to photograph the southwest corner of the Institute building through the laboratory window. It was a bright clear day, the time 1: 30 p.m., the date October 9, 1924. I used a 4x5 par speed portrait cut film and the exposure was half a second, the aperture f/16. Translated into present terminology, the film speed would approximate ASA 2, as compared to modern films which are often several hundred times faster. Making use of the increased film speeds, on the one hand, and artificial light sources especially designed for taking pictures indoors, on the other, resulted in an enormously expanded interest and activity in photography. Two powerful light sources of very short duration, namely the aluminum foil photoflash lamp and the electronic flash, commonly known as strobe, which came into being in 1931 and 1937 respectively, brought a new dimension to the photography of subjects in motion.

I was very friendly, very close, to a family which was musical, and this was the elder daughter of the house playing Bach on her cello. It was my first experiment in recording a moving subject with aluminum foil photoflash lamps, newly arrived from Germany where they had been invented in 1931. The picture was taken by firing one lamp during the open and close shutter movement. At that time, since I was a student in photography and I read everything and saw everything that was being done, I was strictly a Westonian. The creed was that photography was a way of communicating—I don't want to use the word art—and you communicate something novel through texture, and it is the contrast between the adjacent areas that gives you the shock and the impact. Well now, I love this, and I've kept it all these years, because, I suppose, I was romantically attached, not to the girl, but to the idea of music. I found the photograph very satisfying, but I kept wishing it was sharper. This necessity for sharpness of detail, which is after all the prime requisite for photographic quality, led shortly to the development of synchronizers. These made possible photoflash exposures of 1/100 to 1/250 of a second duration. The portrait of a laughing fellow engineer, my first attempt in the use of a synchronizer, shows a distinct improvement in capturing a full laugh without blurring or loss of detail.

Margaret Aue playing cello, 1931.

Between 1928 and 1929 I was a lighting research engineer with the Westinghouse Lamp Division. Then in 1937 I came to give a lecture at M.I.T. before a symposium of the engineering societies. I was asked to speak about existing light sources in photography. The other speaker on that occasion was Dr. Harold E. Edgerton of M.I.T.; he talked about his recent development of an electronic flash, with the remarkably short duration of 1/100,000 of a second, which had allowed him to make some extraordinary photographs.

After the meeting he said, "Come, I want to talk to you." Back in his office he asked, "What can we do with this light source, from your

Man laughing, 1931.

point of view?" I said, "Give me ten times the light, and I quit West-inghouse!" Professor Edgerton agreed to furnish me with a battery of his lights to test their use in actual commerce. You see, by this time *Life* had been created. For the previous three or four years I had been a consultant in establishing the techniques for color and flash photography. I even had the run of Steichen's studio. Every time Steichen had a problem in lighting he picked up the phone and said come over and how do we resolve this or that. I was fortunate to have started early enough in photography to have gotten the basic background for resolving these problems. Well, six months later, I had five times the light from Edgerton and we had an assist from Agfa. Agfa put out a film, the first super pan film, which was three times as fast as anything that we had. Agfa took it in one jump to ASA 32. Well, I was in business. I spent about six months doing experimental photographs, and then I went to *Life*.

Bobby Riggs, 1938.

Don McNeil, 1940.

September 4, 1938; my first assignment from *Life:* Bobby Riggs, the tennis champion. Photographs of his three strokes: serve, forehand and backhand. When these pictures were published everybody was startled to see the ball stopped sharp in mid-air. Notice the contortions of the muscles. But now I find this photograph weak, dated; the ball appears inactive.

Two years later I photographed Riggs' successor, Don McNeil, and got a proper shot where body, facial expression, racket, and ball combine effectively.

Celestine Jay Ku, "Blowing Bubbles,"
1941

A photograph need not invite reflection
so much as create a shock and arouse
the viewer to the strangeness of the
passage. It can illuminate the truth of
a gesture, make visual a musician making music. It can give life to stone, capture the wonder of a child reaching for
a soap bubble.

Carol Lynne, 1945.

In 1949 I was asked to do Picasso's portrait for *Life.* I said, "All right, how
do you get to him?" Well, I even asked
Matisse. I said, "Can you get me an
introduction to Picasso?" He said, "No
you have to go to the beach." Well that I
knew as much. But on my way through
Paris to the Riviera, I stopped to meet
one of his nephews, Javier Vilate, a
young painter. I spent an evening with
him and one thing he said struck a re-
sponsive chord in my mind: "My uncle
says, 'If you want to draw, you must
shut your eyes and sing.' " That went
through my mind all the way from
Paris to the Riviera. I thought, why not
draw in the dark, but with a light instead of a pencil? Days later, settled at
Golfe Juan near the beach where Picasso swam daily, I observed him from
a distance for a full morning. I got the
routine of his movements precisely.
The next day when he was about to
leave, and I could tell, I just dropped
right in his way . . . he's very short.
I said, "Excuse me, I'm a photographer.
I would like to do your portrait." He
said, "Oh? Go ahead." I said, "No,
serious, serious." And at that point I
confronted him with a photograph,
taken in darkness, showing a skater's
spread leap traced with lights attached
to the skates. Picasso reacted instantly.

Picasso's first attempt at drawing in space with light, 1949.

Being able to make an image of your fellow man in a way that is distinctive and at the same time illuminating is about the finest thing that you can do. Ideally the candid portrait should capture a distinctive facet of character so vividly as to shock the viewer. A moment can hardly reveal the whole person but it can communicate one of two things: the emotional state of the subject, or a dominant, not necessarily definable expression that is characteristic of the person.

I was on the French Riviera taking publicity photographs for a film, *Lady L,* with Sophia Loren and Paul Newman. Well, I was there for a week or two and you know you have to make friends. Fortunately I had assistance from another photographer who had done work with me. An Italian boy said, "Do you mind if I follow you? I want to see what you do." (He was a paparazzo). I said, "Sure." You see, Sophia Loren is Eisenstadt's property; we split the world in fiefs, so to speak. So one bright morning at nine, which was very early for Madame, I just came out with a camera. "What are you trying to do?" she protested, "No, no, no. Darling, it's too early in the morning!" And her hand shot out to shield her face from the camera. Now truth to tell, I was not sure that I had a photograph, but fortunately the teeth and the eye breaking through the open fingers are enough to indicate the rambunctious, vital quality, well, the *femaleness* of the lady.

Raoul Dufy paints a church at Rock-port, Massachusetts, August, 1949.

Sometimes the simple matter of taking a portrait can result in a heartwarming tale. A photograph of Raoul Dufy painting, which appeared in *Life* magazine (December 12, 1949), was instrumental in bringing him to America, under the auspices of the Arthritic Foundation, to seek a cure for his advanced arthritis with the newly discovered drug, cortisone. In short, his condition improved substantially in a matter of months, his spirits rose, and I acquired one fine friend.

Anthony Blum, solo, "Dancers at a Gathering," (Jerome Robbins), 1969.

The four consecutive images of the dancer performing were impressed on the same frame of film with electronic flashes. Fired at will as the dance evolved, they created this unique, never-to-be-duplicated pattern.

Group, "Dancers at a Gathering," (Jerome Robbins), 1969.

I had no particular reason to start learning photography. In high school I was living in Rumania and photography was really very primitive. I remember experimenting with one of my friends in high school, copying photographs: printing them from negatives. It was a matter of putting paper against the negative on the window in the sun and doing it for something like a minute or two before you had an image, and movies to me were the *Perils of Pauline* . . . .

By and large my engineering training reduced photography to an exercise in logic and legibility; I had to have a good reason for making a photograph and I had to know how to resolve my technical problems so that the image would speak clearly. This way of thinking made it easy for me to accept Edward Weston's belief that the camera should be used for rendering the very substance and quintessence of *the thing itself*, whether it be polished steel or palpitating flesh. Sharply drawn texture was a technical necessity, and presenting enhanced reality, freezing the moment, seemed sufficient unto itself. But in time, I felt this approach limiting, and I found myself doing more and more interpretive reporting of humanistic subjects. Little did I realize that, in losing part of the contents of my studio unexpectedly through a fire, I would gain a freer, if more complex, vision.

It was not until 1969, when I photographed Jerry Robbins' ballet "Dancers at a Gathering," that I purposely let chance, unshaped elements become part of the composition. Concurrently with the precisely conceived strobe sequences, which had become a trademark of my work, I also registered on the same piece of film the random imagery that occurs with normal lighting when the camera is open for seconds at a time. What pleases me is that somehow or other, partly due to the ballet sense which I had acquired through continuously photographing and viewing ballet, partly due to luck, I was able to keep coherence within my patterns. More often than not the photographs we consider best seem largely accidental. It is as if a combination of unforeseen circumstances had joined to create a unique moment, never to be realized again. The image which ensues still may not necessarily have the clarity, the sharpness of an instantaneous image, but a coherent pattern sometimes spells more than sheer reality. In other words, I was trying to poeticize with the camera. I always start with preconceived notions, which serve as guideposts. I once went into the theatre during a final rehearsal and pointed the camera at the dancers as they were moving with the lighting, and opened the camera for half a second, for a second, to see what I would get. But what I did there was to move the camera in hand, not hold it steady, but move it in counterpoint to the movement hoping that whenever there was a rest in movement in the subject, in the ballet, my hand would also be steadfast, and so I would get an occasional sharp image which would counterbalance the sense of movement which is not clarified otherwise. Experience has taught me what Heraclitus knew already: "If you do not expect it, you will not find the unexpected, for it is hard to find and difficult." I often say to students that sometimes it's ambiguity that creates the photograph.

There is something about this which, frankly, defies the laws of probability. So to me these are all accidents. I'm not concerned with art, really; I'm concerned with photography, whatever it may be. I didn't come here as a photographer; I came here as a humanist. Teaching you photography would be a failure. How can you teach something that took me fifty years to learn and forget? You can't teach that sort of thing in life.

51 GJON MILI

Robert
Frank

Robert Frank was born in Zurich, Switzerland, in 1924. He began to photograph in 1942, and served apprenticeships with Hermann Eidenberg in Basel, and Michael Wolgensinger in Zurich. In 1947, Frank came to the United States and worked as a fashion photographer for *Harper's Bazaar,* with the encouragement of Alexey Brodovitch. In 1948, Frank spent six months traveling in Bolivia and Peru. Photographs from the trip were first published in *Neuf,* 1952, and later published as the book, *Incas to Indians,* with additional photographs by Werner Bischof and Pierre Verger. In 1953, Frank accompanied Edward Steichen to Europe for a collection trip leading to the exhibition, "Post-War European Photographers," and in 1955 became the first European to receive a Guggenheim Fellowship. Under the Guggenheim Fellowship, Frank traveled and photographed in the United States, and published *Les Américains,* with an introduction by Alain Bosquet (Paris, 1958), and *The Americans,* with an introduction by Jack Kerouac. Frank began filmmaking in 1958, and he recently completed a film on The Rolling Stones.

I'm just trying to, as they say, find my bearings. But what shall we talk about? I usually talk about the weather first. I live in Nova Scotia now, and one thing it has done to me is I changed speed. It's a remote little village—Cape Breton, and it's very slow. Once I got stuck in a field with the truck, and a guy I know stopped on the road and came walking over. He just looked at me and said, "Calm down, Robert. Calm down." That's sort of one change I felt by living there, but I think that's a very important change. I calmed down.

I was apprenticed in Switzerland when I was nineteen or so, to a photographer, and switched to some others. I did it mainly because I didn't want to go into my father's business. I had no Brownie, you know, or anything. I never went to photography school, but I was lucky in meeting the right people. In New York. That's what New York is great for. You really meet the people you need. You choose them. I lived in New York for a long time, and I think it wore me down. I didn't want to fight that hard anymore. I sort of ran away. I still think New York is an incredible place, and that I could go back and work there again, because in Nova Scotia I wasn't able to work.

Now I'm in California, teaching filmmaking for two months at the University of California at Davis. I like that, because I can talk about filmmaking quite easily—it's easier than talking about photography, because photography is sort of in the past for me, and I always like to talk about what happens now.

Why did you leave still photography to do film?

It was logical for me to get off doing still photography and becoming a success at it. I think it would just become a repeat—I would repeat myself. I have found my style, and I could build on that, and just sort of vary it a little bit here and there. But beyond that, I don't think there's much beyond that. I've never been successful at making films, really. I've never been able to do it right. And there's something terrific about that. There's something good about being a failure—it keeps you going. I mean, you look for it, to do it right; and I felt I wouldn't spend that much energy or that much effort in still photography anymore. Well, you repeat yourself anyhow. There are a few essential ideas that an artist has, and you work with them all your life. I think you have to make a conscious effort to at least get off of it a little bit. You will always come back to it. I have a lot of good ideas sometimes, but I forget some of them, or they get mixed up by becoming verbalized.

Probably another reason I moved away from still photography is because I do a lot of things intuitively. I felt I would get caught up in being kind of analytical, and building onto it and perfecting it. I didn't want to go on. I didn't want to hear about it anymore. As it turned out, once I turned away from still photography, everybody got really interested in me, and why I turned away from it. But the fact that I don't do it anymore has to do with my temperament. It has to do with my curiosity. I believe very much that an artist has to be very curious. I mean about other things.

As a still photographer I wouldn't have to talk to anyone. I could walk around and not say anything. You're just an observer; you just walk around, and there's no need to communicate. And so you feel that you don't have to use words. Whereas with films it becomes more complicated—thinking in long durations, and keeping up a kind of sequence.

I began filmmaking right after *The Americans*—1959. This guy said, "Let's go down to Florida with a camera—a 16mm camera—and you make a little film there, like your photographs." So I went down there, and I shot about fifteen rolls, about a half hour's worth of film. And then I came back to New York and I didn't have any money to develop it, and I put it away. I kept thinking about what I had done down there, and it's funny. I thought, "I've done the same thing as I did in the photographs. I photographed the same scenes and the same people." I have never developed the stuff. I just thought a lot about it. It was a terrific lesson, and I think it taught me that I didn't want at all to make a film that would look like my photographs—that would have any connection with them. That was probably not too good a decision right away, because that's when all the failures came marching in. I mean, I thought I could work with actors, which I couldn't. So maybe it would have been better if I had made some kind of documentary films in the beginning.

Are you satisfied with your failures in film?

I'm satisfied that I've done them. I guess I would have been happier if they had been successful, but I believe very strongly, the main thing is to do it. I just looked at a film that I'd done maybe five or six years ago. It was a film called *Life Raft Earth* which was a straight documentary on a demonstration in California, organized by the *Whole Earth Catalogue* people. They fasted for many days in a parking lot. I didn't like the film too well after I finished it—I thought it not very well photographed. And now I like it quite a bit. I thought it was very valuable to me. I'd made a record of what happened, and I think that way it's satisfying. Even a failure can be quite important, and maybe it will turn around and not be such a failure. After all, when the book *The Americans* first came out, it wasn't very well received at all. They wouldn't publish it. They thought it was terrible—anti-American, un-American, dirty, overexposed, crooked.

Did you have the same experience with the book as you did with the film—sort of stepping back after a few years and feeling better about it?

No, I was sure about the book. But with the films, I'm never sure. Well, I've made a film about the Rolling Stones and the tour, and that's a film I feel pretty sure about. I feel it's true. You know, when you do something, you have to feel that. I knew the photographs were true. They were what I felt, they were completely intuitive. There was no thinking. That feeling has stayed with me; I never waivered from that.

When I did *The Americans* I was very ambitious. I knew I wanted to do a book, and I was deadly serious about it, and somehow things just happened right. It was the first time I had seen this country, and it was the right mood. I had the right influences—I knew Walker's photographs, I knew what I didn't want, and then that whole enormous country sort of coming against my eyes. It was a tremendous experience, and I worked, but it came naturally to show what I felt, seeing those faces, those people, the kind of hidden violence. The country at that time—the McCarthy period—I felt it very strongly.

Walker Evans, *Outdoor Advertising Sign near Baton Rouge, Louisiana,* 1935.

Robert Frank, *Covered Car, Long Beach, California,* **The Americans,** 1959.

There were a lot of juke-boxes in *The Americans.* **Were they an intentional symbol of the fifties?**

I guess it was something new that I had never seen, really, and I was impressed with that. I think I like pictures that would convey a sound. Maybe it has something to do with that. You would look at the photographs, and maybe you would hear the sound come out. I don't know, but probably it was like a symbol that I saw over and over again. I like the picture that has the television set in it. I think I always like pictures that have that element in it—that you would hear the sound, or imagine the sound.

Somebody asked me the other day why I never talked about what happened to me on that trip. I never really did, and it was sort of

Robert Frank, *Drive-In Movie, Detroit,*
The Americans, 1959.

curious that I never talked about it, so I told them a few things. Like
in McGee, Arkansas, you know, they arrested me. I was driving early
in the morning on a little country road, and the cops came, stopped
my car, and said, "What are you doing?" I said, "I'm on a Guggenheim Fellowship, and I'm traveling around photographing the country." The guy said, "Guggenheim? Who is that?" So they pulled me
in. They said, "We got to arrest you," and I said, "What for?" and
they said, "Never mind," and kept me in jail for almost three days. I
didn't know anybody; they could have killed me. It's pretty scary, and
I think that somehow came through in the photographs—that violence I was confronted with. Besides that, I had the influence of *Life*
magazine. I wanted to sell my pictures to them, and they never did
buy them. So I developed a tremendous contempt for them, which
helped me.

How did that contempt for *Life* help you?

As an artist today I somehow feel that you have to be enraged. I
mean, besides the intuition I had and how the country affected me,
I also didn't want to produce what everybody else was producing. I
wanted to follow my own intuition and do it my way, and not make
any concession—not make a *Life* story. That was another thing I
hated. Those goddamned stories with a beginning and an end.

Are you still enraged?

No, I think your rage goes down comparatively as you get older. The
only photographer that I think has steadily shown new work and
good work is Bill Brandt. But most of the great photographers, like
Cartier-Bresson—compared to his early work—the work in the past
twenty years, well, I would rather he hadn't done it. That may be too
harsh, but I've always thought it was terribly important to have a
point of view, and I was always sort of disappointed in him that that
was never in his pictures. He traveled all over the goddamned world,
and you never felt that he was moved by something that was happening other than the beauty of it, or just the composition. That's certainly why *Life* gave him big assignments. They knew he wouldn't
come up with something that wasn't acceptable.

Robert Frank, **The Lines of My Hand,**
1972.

Robert Frank, *Filmstrip, Me and My
Brother, 1965-68,* **The Americans,** 1969,
2nd ed.

I remember *Life* once gave me an assignment. I went with Kerouac to pick up his mother. We wanted to get some money for the trip to Florida, so I said, "Let's get some money from *Life.*" We went there, and they said, "Alright, Kerouac will write a story, and you'll photograph." So we did it, and I showed them the photographs, and the guy said, "Well, this looks like Russia." I never forgot that.

How did *Lines of My Hand* come about? Were you moved by this same contempt for *Life*?

There's a Japanese edition of that book that explains it very well. These two Japanese came, whom I'd never seen before, and they said, "We want to do a book of your photographs." We became quite good friends—we have a correspondence, and I felt I really wanted to give them something that would tell them about myself. So they made a book that's a little bit different than the American edition—it's a very expensive book: it's big and elaborate, and it's much better than the American edition. But then again, it's a book that goes back. It's all looking back. And I don't want to do it anymore.

Are you bored with stills?

Well, I looked at the exhibition here; somehow boredom is a rough word to use. I looked at Mili's stuff, and that certainly bores me. I liked what Smith wrote about the photographs—why he photographs, what he believes. I wouldn't be bored with him because he's obsessed with it. I'm never bored when I feel an obsession in somebody. I'm bored with the aesthetics of photographs, but then I think Walker's photographs are like jewels. They stay the same. I'm not bored with that. I'm trying to define how I am bored with photographs. I'm sort of bored with mine.

If I continued with still photography, I would try to be more honest and direct about why I go out there and do it. And I guess the only way I could do it is with writing. I think that's one of the hardest things to do—combine words and photographs. But I would certainly try it. It would probably fail; I have never liked what I wrote about my photographs yet. That would be the only way I could justify going out in the streets and photographing again.

Does the film medium allow you to be more "honest and direct"?

I think film is more of a living thing—more of an instant communication between people. If I were to show a film, it would be a very definite statement. That just appeals to me more now—to have that immediate response. Photographs leave too much open to bullshit. There's too much aesthetics involved—too much peripheral talk. I would go out, and I would photograph, and I would come and put the photographs, like twenty of them, on the table here. And you could look at them, and you could pick up more than two, or the whole thing, and nothing definite could be said about them right away. There would be these discussions; you know—it's a good print, or this photograph is good after this one. You can look between the photographs, and I can talk about them and influence you while you're looking. I would never talk while the film runs. Everybody has to look at the film the same way—you have to sit in a dark room, and there's no way out. You either close your eyes or look at it. And it isn't anymore a question of whether the photograph is good or bad. It's whether I got through with that film what I wanted to say.

Do you think that it has something to do with the fact that film is a couple of more elements closer to how we experience life—in that it has movement, and it has sound? That it's more complex?

I would just call it truer. It's more stepping in. That's one thing I found in my films. Although it's true that I often feel like an observer, I'm still in it. I'm part of it, definitively. And it's hard to see what part you're in as a photographer. I think Smith is a good example. He is in it. His obsession—I feel that in his photographs. But for ninety-nine per cent of the photographers it's a game. A game with aesthetics or taste, or artistry like Gibson, or jokes like Erwitt, tricks like Mili, fashion like Penn. I mean who else? Name somebody and I'll say something nasty about them. Only the people who are obsessed should continue with photography. Arbus—she was obsessed with her life. A girl I met in New York, a student of Arbus, said to me, "Well you know, I really got mad at Diane Arbus, because she treated our photographs just like she treated the people she photographed. We would put our picture up on the wall and Diane would look at the picture, and she would say, 'Oh, how interesting. Where did you meet that woman, and where did she come from, and what's going on here?'" And the girl was very pissed. She said, "I didn't get anything from her." And I found that very strange. I mean, that's the way Arbus was. That's what got her to get these pictures of these people. It's that curiosity that one has to have.

Anybody who is going to be an artist has to be curious. He's got to go out and do his own thing. If you talk to a student, and the student is any good, has any guts, he will not do what you tell him. And it usually works out that those students are the ones that you really get interested in, and they will get something from you. That's the way I can help as a teacher. I can help those few.

When students bring in their films, I can put my finger on something important right away that goes on inside them. The films are somehow more revealing than photographs. It's because the film-maker cannot get away with that instant that might be accidental. He's got to come up with three minutes, and you see there how he feels, how he goes back, how he looks away, how he runs to something else, or how confused he is looking around. And the same thing happens when I show my movies—the personal movies that deal with my life. I've done two or three of them, and after the light goes on and I'm out there, I really feel like I've taken my clothes off, in a way. I feel like I've really shown a lot. And some people understand it, and some people don't. But I've never felt that as a photographer. I've never felt like I've given that much. And in a way, that's one thing teaching taught me—to be more generous with myself.

How do you teach film?

We just make films. That's all I'm interested in. I can't just sit there and talk. I give the students a theme. I say, "Make a film about oranges." So they think about it, and some write a script or a little story board, some just go out, some don't know and just sit there and look at you. Or I make a film. Like I said, "I'm going to make a film, and I'm going to title it '1981 Viet Orphans.'" I got to know an eight-year-old half-Chinese boy, and I sat him on a table. I explained to the students what I would do—I just made it up. I gave the boy a big knife, and so this guy's cutting all the vegetables I have there, asparagus, everything. He's just hacking this food apart. I guess this runs about three minutes, and that's the film I made. I haven't gotten it back, but I'll put it on the projector, look at it, and we'll talk about it. The boy got really furious, and that's where I wanted the film to go.

Today you can go out and buy your capsule, your cartridge of Super-8 film for three dollars and fifty cents, put it in your camera, and shoot your stuff. You bring it to the drugstore and it comes back in three days, and you look at it. It's like you use a pencil: you write down what you feel, what you think. Then you can talk about it. Then I can explain about the cutting, and say, "Why did you do it that way? I would do it this way." But what I teach really is to pick up the camera and have the confidence to say something you feel strongly about.

I've thought a lot about teachers—people who teach photography, people who have tenure from colleges. I've been thinking a lot about Callahan. I wonder about anybody that teaches for that long. I don't see how you can keep it up. You must become very uninspired by it. If you're an artist, I think that the university world is not good. I think the real world is better. You have to be against the system in some way. How do you do that? That's the question. You're not going to do it here, or in any school. That much I know. Because this is where the system is taught, and you're a part of it, and I'm a part of it. And I don't want to be a part of it. But I'm here. I'm being paid. And that's my thing; that's the whole thing that I have to offer—that I wasn't part of it. I'm just trying to tell you here what makes me tick. What else am I going to do? Theorize about black and white values?

I just feel that the universities are really very protected compounds or factories, or whatever, and that's why I wonder about Callahan. He keeps on working, and produces that good work. But maybe the work isn't good at all, because he's made this carefully planned move, and he's just perfecting something which is his own vision. And he's perfecting it so beautifully because he's in that beautifully perfected place to begin with. And I hate that. I wish that he would photograph something else. I've seen a show at the Light Gallery, and it's quite beautiful. He prints quite nicely. But I found it deadly. Not in a good way. But I'm not talking against him. It's the aesthetics of tombstone photography.

Do you think that photography today has become overrun by aesthetics?

No, I think a lot of young people have turned away from that. I know a number of young people who photograph and there are no aesthetics involved—they take pictures without looking in the viewfinder. It's just gotta be done. They often don't develop it, but it's something they carry with them, and when they feel like it, they take a few pictures. Maybe later on they'll take them out and do something with them. I think eventually some body of work will come out anyhow, that will express something very strong. Maybe it will take longer, but they're not in a hurry that way.

But then they're not obsessed, either.

Well, that's true, but I think it will come later. I think it's good that today people do a lot of different things—study architecture, or play music, or write a book. And I like it very much when people write with photographs. That's a very hard thing to do. When I started to use the Super-8mm camera, I took footage, and I'd often run the whole film through the camera. Then I'd wind the film back, and then I'd write some sentences on black acetate—just burn it out. I'd put it on a light box, and I'd put that film back that I'd run backwards, and I'd sort of know what was on the film, and I'd put sentences over the whole picture. I mean, it's sort of a destroyed picture. I did that for a while, and I sort of liked it. Those films are somehow simple, like exercises. They're just takes, and they're very satisfying, and in that way they might be like photographs. I put them away and didn't look at them for three years, and they were very true. Those sentences made a lot of sense later. I guess a lot of photography today deals with your personal life. It records it in some way—what you see, or your environment or travels. It's not so much that you want to make beautiful photographs. It's something else, and *that* appeals to me.

I'm not interested in taking a beautiful photograph. I don't mean that there's no room for it; I just don't want to do it. For example, I live in a very beautiful place. I could get a camera, and make a very beautiful picture. It could be almost as good as Ansel Adams. But I don't want to take a beautiful picture, and I can't, really. It makes me feel good to look at it. It wouldn't make me feel good to take that picture.

I don't believe in it anymore—beauty, aesthetics. I think it is crazy if you are a photographer, and the only idea that you have is that you want to be an artist. And that's what I would object to in somebody like Ralph Gibson. That is transparent in his work—wanting to make "art." Every picture is "art": meaning, depth, space, all these words. And some photographs are quite beautiful and memorable. To me photography is life. It has to deal with life. And there's another thing —"good" or "bad." Maybe one shouldn't make any distinction between film and photography when talking about it. You know, it's "good" photography—maybe it's just important to do it. It's important to do a film; it's probably harder to do that. It means more thinking, more preparation. When you do photographs, you can go around, put it together after two years, send out all the postcards, and put it on the wall. Like in the Stones film, it was either do it or get out. Often photography can be in-between, either-or.

I've done Nova Scotia with the movie camera. I've gone from left to right, when it snowed, when it hailed and then when the wind was blowing, and I plan to use that in some way. It's not the beautiful photograph. It just means a passage of time to me. I'm working on a film about my daughter, and another friend of mine who died, and I plan to use that, like time is going by. But I mean, it's beautiful to be alive, but life isn't that beautiful.

In an interview with Walker Evans, you talked about DeKooning and Kline, and the energy that was in New York in the fifties with the abstract expressionists. Do you feel that this sort of energy is necessary for a lot of people to get together and make a movement?

Sometimes, you know, what I'm talking about is not what I mean. But I was talking about a lifestyle that impressed me. It was like a political stand. At that time I think the abstract painters were suffering. They were having a hard time. And they totally believed in what they were doing. They were a really strong group. All that photographers talked about at that time was how to make money, how to get into magazines. It was a relief to go into a group that was not interested

Josef Koudelka, *Okres Hnusta, 1967*, **Gypsies,** 1975.

Walker Evans, *Subway Portrait, 1938-41,* **Many Are Called,** 1966.

Robert Frank, *Funeral, St. Helena, South Carolina,* **The Americans,** 1959.

in that way. And in that way it has changed a lot, because painters have become very successful and very commercial. I have been asked several times to produce a portfolio of my photographs, and I never wanted to, because I somehow am against a certain preciousness. I don't mind if a gallery sells some of my prints, and they go somewhere, and I get some money. But to make a business of it—to print fifty portfolios and sell them for two thousand dollars, and they're all in a box with tissue between them—I don't want to do it. It's deadly. I don't want to have an exhibition, either, because that's deadly too. Museums are . . . well, they're not deadly, but for me it would be back to the old work again. Dig it all up, have it printed up.

Well this museum guy [Szarkowski]—I guess he will be interesting to listen to. I haven't been to the museum in a long time. I like what he's showing now—the Hungarian photographer Koudelka. I'd like to see the Bacon show at the Met. I like his paintings a lot; I get the message. I don't know. The museum is sort of a tastemaker. It's very powerful, and anything that powerful I mistrust in a way.

Well you have your own sense of power, your sense of purity . . .

I think my asset is only that I sort of know who I am. I know what I can do—what I can do well. As an artist, what have you got? No power, nothing. In the end, power I think is measured in dollars. I think of the power that I have encountered in artists that I know. When they get successful, they make factories out of their art. A guy like Indiana, say, builds up his empire. Warhol. I think Warhol is a very important artist; I have great respect for him. The more power you get, you know, it seems the weaker you get as an artist. I often think that the best work you've done is the work you've done when you had no power, really. When you had no name. As a teacher I would just try to get people to get up the courage to do it, not to be afraid that they would fail, just that they tried, that's all. I certainly wouldn't want them to be like me, or make films like me.

Well, feeling like that is part of what people pick up from you, and so that is your influence.

I guess that is powerful, but I never looked at it that way. I'm not conscious of it. Whereas with the Stones, every second, you see that tremendous power that they have. Actually, everybody around them is afraid of them—their friends, everybody. What can they do? They can kill you. It's as simple as that. They can beat you to a pulp and tell you to get out. They can do anything.

How did you go about making the Stones film? Did you get to know them very well before you started shooting?

No, I didn't. I made a record cover for them, and Mick Jagger sort of liked me. They called me up in Nova Scotia. I said to them, "That's the camera I want." They bought the camera, and they said, "You do the film." There was never any more talk about it. I just got paid, and they let me do whatever I wanted to, but it was the agreement that I would finish and give them the film. They have the say whether it's going to come out or not.

We went on tour with them in 1972. It's pretty interesting to get to know somebody as powerful as Jagger, or that group. So much money, so much power. It's sort of frightening. It's a frightening film in that way. And if I could have shown what really went on, it would have been horrendous—not to be believed. The film is a pretty down-trip film. They weren't too happy about it, but Jagger is very straight. He said, "You did the film, that's the way you see it; although that's not the way I see it, that's not the way it really is." I like him personally, and he's quite an amazing guy. He has a fantastic head, and he's really in control. They're rough people to be with. You've got to keep up. If you can't keep up, it's too bad.

You seem to have been a stranger in their world, and there seems to be an element of the stranger in both your films and photography. How do you feel about that?

Well, I think that's quite a good observation. I guess I am an observer, in a way. It also had to do with the fact that a lot of my work deals with myself, especially my films. It's very hard to get away from myself. It seems, almost, that's all I have. That's sort of a sad feeling. But that feeling of being a stranger—it has to do with years of photography, where you walk around, you observe, and you walk away, and you begin to be a pretty good detective.

I was very happy to make the Stones film, because it got me away from myself. But then again, the film turned out to be about my friend. We both made the film together, but he really sort of lived what the Stones imagined they were living. It was a drug scene, but he really did it in front of the camera, and I lived with him, so I made the film on him, part of it. And on Jagger and Richards. Those were the three people that interested me. I wasn't interested in the music at all, I mean the performance, but Jagger knew that. I guess that's one of the reasons he liked me.

You spoke earlier of your mistrust for powerful institutions, like the museum. Do you feel the same sort of mistrust toward Jagger?

There are two images in my mind. On the one hand, I admire him because of his ability as a performer, his capability as an administrator of such a powerful business venture. But then on the other hand, it would be the same for a politician whom I would mistrust. In the end it would turn me off completely. I would have nothing to do with it, because in the end he would destroy me. Because I don't play his game; I'm not in his class. All the personalities in that group are especially rough. They are hard on each other, they are completely without feeling for anyone around them. Anything goes to get the work going and keep it moving. And that's a strong experience to go through—to see that, and how it works.

Well, let's talk about John Morris. I knew Morris from when he was with *Ladies' Home Journal*. He promised me work, and he never gave me work. He said, "Look, I think that you can get into Magnum, and I'm going to bring them all down here." And Cartier-Bresson, and Capa, and Erwitt—they all came down, and they looked at my pictures, and they didn't say much. But then he called me back a few days later, and he said, "Well, we will take you." He lined up an arrangement for me, and I would make a certain amount of money, and I really couldn't have done it. I felt that they didn't really want me, and it was more a personality thing. And he said to me, "You know, you should learn to take more vertical pictures, because we work for magazines." I never forgot that.

You did fashion work, too, didn't you?

When I came here, that was the first job I got. Brodovitch of *Harper's Bazaar* hired me. He was a very important photography teacher at that time, 1948 or 1949, and he had these classes, and he asked me to come. I was very thankful to him, because he got me that job, but I discovered that in his classes, all he wanted to get was ideas for fashion photography—new ideas. And I dropped out right away. I was never any good at fashion photography. I had no interest in clothes, which you have to have if you're a fashion photographer. That was interesting about Brodovitch, that he thought he could make me into a fashion photographer. He had the same idea about Cartier-Bresson.

Can you talk a little about Walker Evans?

Yeah, well, he helped me a lot when I was starting. He helped me get the Guggenheim. He never said much, but he's a guy who doesn't have to say much, but you know he understands what you're about. So we had a good thing that way. He came up to Nova Scotia about three years ago. He had recovered from an operation, and he came up there to visit. I took him to all the old houses—the people live just like in the thirties or forties in the States, and he was overjoyed. He photographed and photographed. And I liked to see him so happy about photographing, but at the same time, I felt that I wouldn't want to do that when I'm older.

I once came to see Walker at the office at *Fortune*. It was when Agee had died, 1955, around the time I got the Guggenheim. Agee was his best friend, and I remember him just sitting on his desk in front of a window and looking down on Rockefeller Center—you know, where they ice skate?—and he just sat there and he cried. I was very moved by it. I went with him on a trip to photograph mills in New England, and his wife had left him, and he was very sad then. He was very intelligent, but he didn't play the intellectual, although I'm sure he had it. He went to very good schools, and he talked a lot about breeding. He had class and style. A lot of California painters are certainly tremendously influenced by Walker's photographs. The whole pop art thing is very strongly influenced by photography.

Walker couldn't stand Steichen. What about Steichen? Do people talk about him? I think he had a terrific understanding about art—painting and sculpture. I think his judgment about that is probably better than about photography. But if there's one thing I dislike in photography, it's sentimentality. And Steichen to me must be—how do you say it?—the personification of sentimentality. I can't stand that.

What do you think of Dorothea Lange's work?

I like her work. I remember, I went to see her when she was very sick, in California, and she sat there in her bed and we talked about things. Then, all of a sudden, she said, "I just photographed you." And you know, I was looking around, and I understood. She took a picture of me in her mind. And that was a very nice thing she said.

My favorite photographers are Bill Brandt, Walker Evans, Dorothea Lange, and I like Emmet Gowin. These are sort of classic photographers, so I'm, you know, I'm an old man. I like the classic stuff.

I can't talk about photographs, really. There's a certain verbal gift you have to have. What could I teach you except to tell you about myself? Whatever help that would be. You know, one of the worst things an artist can do is talk about his work.

65 ROBERT FRANK

Frederick Wiseman

Frederick Wiseman was born in Boston in 1932 and grew up in Brookline, Massachusetts. He graduated from Williams College in 1951 and from Yale Law School in 1954; in 1973 he received an honorary degree in Humane Letters from the University of Cincinnati. He has practiced and taught law in Paris and Massachusetts and is a member of the Massachusetts Bar Association. Since 1967, Wiseman has made ten films as an independent filmmaker, and he is now the General Manager of Zipporah Films, Incorporated, Boston. His films have won numerous awards, and all except *Titicut Follies* and *High School* have been aired on public television. Wiseman's latest film, *Meat,* concerns the day-to-day activities at one of the largest feed lot and packing plants in the country.

For the last nine years, I have been working on a series of films
that are loosely defined as part of an institutional series, with no precise definitions of either institution or series. I became a filmmaker
because the idea had interested me for a long time and I was growing increasingly bored with and indifferent toward practicing and
teaching law. While I was teaching, I used to take students to correc-
tional institutions where their future clients might be sent, and one
of those places was the hospital for the criminally insane at Bridgewater. I vividly remember my first trip to Bridgewater in 1959. I
thought at the time that it might be a good film subject, and it became the subject of my first film *Titicut Follies*.

I had seen so many films that followed one charming individual,
whether it were a movie star or rock star, that I thought it would be
more interesting to make a film in which the place were the star.
Essentially, what I have been doing since then is a form of natural
history. I try to look at what is going on to discover what kind of
power relationships exist and differences between ideology and the
practice in terms of the way people are treated. The theme that
unites the films is the relationship of people to authority.

I pick an institution; by that I mean simply a place that has certain
kinds of geographic limitations and where at least some of the people
have well-established roles. I generally try to select an institution
that is defined as good within the system in which it operates. For
example, in *High School* I deliberately rejected a ghetto or inner city
school because everybody knew they had a lot of problems; rather I
picked a school that turned out to be one of the two best schools in
Philadelphia. The same thing happened in *Titicut Follies,* because
Bridgewater, horrible as it was, was considered one of the better
prisons of its kind in the country. If you don't start with a place that
is defined at least by the world in which it exists as good, then the situation is too easy and not complicated enough to merit a year's work.

Titicut Follies was financed by a lab in New York. A documentary
can cost a lot of money or very little. To keep the cost down, you have
to use the same kind of judgment necessary in any good business
practice. When I began I didn't have any money to lose, in the sense
that if I went into debt, I had the choice of working to pay off the debt
or going bankrupt, and I was willing to take that risk. A lab was willing to gamble with me and gave me credit, a long deferment. In fact,
I didn't pay the lab on the *Follies* for six years; but they were willing
to go along with it because in the meantime I had given them business on my other films. It's not easy, but it's not terribly difficult to get
a lab to go along with you *if* you want to take the risk, which is a
severe one. And if you go bankrupt, which is one way of avoiding
the debt, that's the end of your getting credit in the movie business.
So it's not done lightly.

There's a lot of mystification about movies, a special vocabulary
that takes about twenty-five minutes to learn which people use, just
like any special vocabulary, to exclude other people. The money issue
in film is certainly crucial, but it's sometimes viewed as an obstacle
when it's not, especially since there's so much equipment around.
Many people have Eclairs and Nagras which they're not using most
of the time; you can usually borrow the equipment or rent it for a
small amount of money. People who work or teach in film schools frequently have a lot of equipment available, or you can ask one of the
equipment supply houses in New York who in Boston has recently

bought equipment. In addition, raw stock can be obtained relatively cheaply at, for instance, Defense Department auctions, if you're willing to organize yourself and be a bit of an entrepreneur about wheeling and dealing. You have to be *very aggressive* about all aspects of it; you can then make a film for a relatively small amount of money.

The politics of getting permission is another issue which is sometimes very complicated and sometimes very easy. First I try to find someone within the bureaucracy who wants to have a film made, for reasons that correspond or in some way coincide with my own, who then becomes an internal advisor on how to obtain permission to make the film. He advises me on the initial responses to the request to do the film and tells me whom to see and who has authority to grant permission. I always offer to show any of my earlier films. Although I would like to think that everybody has seen the films and knows about them, the fact of the matter is that most of the people of whom I ask permission have never heard of me nor seen any of my films. It seems perfectly natural that somebody would want to see what I've done elsewhere, but it's very rare that that happens. The only time my offer was taken up in any detail was with the Army. They saw everything I had done before they gave me permission to make *Basic Training*.

Why I get permission, or why anybody gets permission, I don't really know. I think it's a combination of passivity and vanity, primarily vanity in that people are flattered that you're interested in spending the time to photograph and record what they're doing, and that their work will be presented on public television.

After having been granted permission, I write a letter to the head of the institution outlining what I plan to do. Since I don't know in advance exactly what will happen in the course of filming, I can't say definitely what the final film will be, particularly since none of the events are staged. I list as examples events that I think might happen. In the same letter I also make clear that I have editorial control over the film.

Before I begin filming, I usually spend a day or two trying to get a sense of the place and particularly trying to find those people who are making decisions and who have power over others. I don't believe in doing much research beyond that because, in a sense, the shooting of the film is the research. There are usually no books that have been written about the particular place where I'm making the film, and in any event, I was a very bad student in foreign languages in college and so I have a great deal of difficulty in reading in the social sciences. Instead, I try to find some novels that are more or less directed to the subject of the film to get a sense of what someone else thought about a similar place. Usually, either the day I start, or the day before, I have a notice placed on the bulletin boards so that as many people as possible have access to information that a film is being made, and so that everybody doesn't stop us in the corridor to ask what the camera and tape recorder are for. If possible I may also have the institution's bulletin or newsletter publish a notice about the film.

Once you start shooting, you use a combination of judgment, luck and good informants. I use informants in the best sense of the word because I am very dependent on people within the institution to tell me what's going on and what they think is relevant since I really don't know that much about it. For example, I relied on the

Frederick Wiseman, *Dean of Discipline Punishing Student,* **High School,** 1968.

Dean of Discipline in *High School* because he came up to me the
first day that I was there and said, "You ought to come to my office
at 9:15 in the morning and see the culprits line up outside the door."
That was a very inviting suggestion, so the next morning I went
down and the culprits, about twenty of them, were lined up outside
the door. Then his office became a difficult place to stay away from.
It was a particularly significant place to be, not only for its situation
comedy value, but also because the Dean of Discipline felt compelled
to rationalize to the students the reasons for whatever particular
punishment he was giving, revealing as he did so, some of the values
and ideologies of the institution. Similarly, a student came up to me
one day and said that I ought to come to his English class because
he thought he had a good English teacher, and it turned out to be
the teacher who read "Casey at the Bat." These are only two examples of what happens all the time.

The basic technique in filming is to hang around with a tape
recorder and a 16mm Eclair camera. All the equipment is hand held.
There are no artificial lights; you use natural lights and very fast
black and white Kodak double-x 72/22 film. I think black and white
film is more appropriate than color for these particular subjects. To
get good color, you would have to use lights and really control the
light, which you really can't do in this type of filming. For example,
an ambulance pulls up outside Metropolitan Hospital; somebody
comes crashing down the corridor in a stretcher. You don't know
which of the six emergency rooms you're going to go to, and even if
you did, you wouldn't know quite how the people were going to be
placed and, therefore, how you should light the room. A lot of extra
lights would make people too self-conscious. Black and white is more
appropriate for the look I want the film to have.

I don't do the shooting myself. I direct and do the sound, and work
with a cameraman. There are certain kinds of things you have to
have in every situation; you've got to have wide shots, you've got to
follow the action which means following whoever is talking, and
you've got to shoot for cutaways. I'm much freer to see what's going

on because I'm not shooting. The cameraman has got one eye on the viewfinder and one eye on me, and I've got one eye on him and one eye on what's going on. When it works it's like a little dance because we're moving around the people that we're shooting; and at the same time we have our own little signals for each other. My instinct is always to shoot. Once you think something is okay you shoot even though it might turn out to be no good because you can never predict how an event will turn out. In the long run, it is really more economical to take the risk of shooting, ending up with a thirty to one ratio, than to try to control it more completely and only shoot, say ten to one, and not spend as much money. With a smaller ratio you won't have as good a film because you won't have the range of choices that you need in the editing. You shoot a lot of little incidental things which you really don't yet know how you're going to use, but you know they're going to be useful. You try to get as much of the general activity as you can, not following any particular theory except for your own instinct of what appears to be interesting, relevant or amusing.

I don't really think the presence of the camera affects people's behavior because I don't think any of us has the capacity to suddenly change our behavior and become something we're not. If we did have that talent, we'd all be in the Old Vic, and most of us aren't such good actors. I think that if the camera equipment makes people nervous, the chances are that rather than try something new, they'll fall back on forms of behavior they're comfortable with, that they think are appropriate and natural for the situation. For example, in *Law and Order* there's a sequence in which a cop finds a girl accused of prostitution in the basement of a hotel. There was no light at all in the cellar, so we had to use a sungun. In front of the camera, the sungun and the tape recorder the cop proceeded to strangle her, finally letting her go just before she passed out. After she pulled herself together she said to the cop, "You were trying to strangle me!", and another cop said, "Oh, you're just imagining that." Now you could presumably argue that had the camera not been there he might have

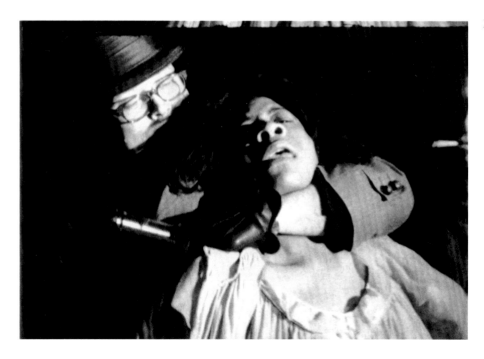

Frederick Wiseman, **Law and Order,** 1969.

killed her, but I don't think so. I think that he just felt that it was an appropriate way to behave toward the girl.

A documentary filmmaker is no different from anyone who meets a lot of people in the course of his work. To survive you have to develop a sensitive bullshit meter. If you think someone is conning you or putting it on for the camera, you stop shooting. And if you only realize it in the editing, you don't use the footage. You're not always right, but it's an issue that you have to be very aware of.

After a month or so of shooting, you may accumulate forty to fifty hours of footage which will be edited to a film of perhaps eighty or ninety minutes. It takes four to five weeks to synchronize the sound and picture tracks after you return from shooting. While you're doing that, you make up three by five cards or a notebook indexing what's on every roll. By the time you finish, you know the material reasonably well. Then you make up an outline against which you work. During that process, you probably discard, at least temporarily, about sixty percent of the material. At this point, I try to make a list of those sequences which I think will be major to the film and I begin to think about their relationship to each other.

Since the themes of a documentary evolve from the experience of shooting and editing the material, you have to think through what each sequence means to you in order to figure out whether to use it or whether part of it will fit in the film. That is essentially what's involved in the editing because you haven't had time to do that while shooting. In the end there must be a rationale for why each segment is where it is, what it's relationship is to the sequence before and after and to the overall themes that are being developed.

In the process of editing I have left out sequences that might have been good, not because they were too shocking or too emotionally charged, but because they would have "loaded" the film too much. For example, in *High School* the teacher who reads "Casey at the Bat" gave a multiple choice test on *Hamlet* a few days later that went something like: Hamlet loves Polonius, hates Polonius, is indifferent to Polonius, check one. I thought that would be a bit unfair. I like "Casey at the Bat" better and couldn't use them both.

The film begins to emerge only toward the last three or four weeks of editing. Material which you originally thought useless usually saves the film because it provides you with the cutaways, or pauses, or whatever. For example, toward the end of the editing of *Hospital,* I was concerned about the pacing of the film because I felt there were too many big sequences too close to each other. I had not yet used a series of corridor sequences, people hanging around in the corridor or stretchers being taken down corridors, or ambulances arriving. When they were put into the film they provided pauses between the long scenes, as well as some action which gave a rhythm or pace to the material that it previously didn't have.

High School took me the least amount of time to edit—four months, and *Primate* the most—fourteen months. One of the things I was trying to do in *Primate* was to see to what extent you could tell the story just by pictures. There was very little dialogue in *Primate.* In most of my films there are about ninety pages of dialogue and in *Primate* there are thirty-two.

Primate begins with shots of the government behaviorists and ends with a space trip. There is a connection to be made between that kind of research and that kind of result. One of the interesting

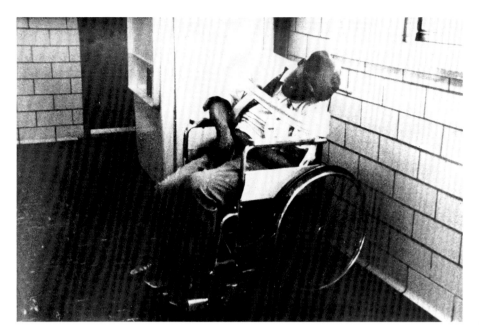

Frederick Wiseman, *Drunken Man
Tied to Wheelchair to Keep Him from
Falling on the Floor,* **Hospital,** 1970.

things about Yerkes is that it provides the opportunity to see the ap-
plication of the scientific method in two crucial kinds of situations
involving both behavioral and biological problems. And you see in
the film some of the implications of both kinds of research. One of the
curious things about *Primate* is that in many ways the concerns of
the scientists are exactly the same issues that concern the teachers in
High School, namely, how to control sexual and aggressive behavior.
I think my point of view is very strongly revealed in *Primate,* but it's
revealed structurally in the arrangement of the sequences.

Some documentary filmmakers don't feel you should edit at all.
I'm very much more interested in form than some other filmmakers,
and in tight control of the material. The whole effort is an attempt to
assert some kind of control over chaos. The form of the film is totally
fictional but it's based on a reality situation. A sequence in real time
might last an hour and a half of which you shoot fifty minutes and
end up using only three. That three minutes may come from the first,
the thirtieth and fortieth minute of the sequence. You are able to link
those three bits of dialogue together by use of cutaways. The result
is a sequence which is totally arbitrary in that it never existed in real
life, but it works in film terms. All the material is manipulated so that
the final film is totally fictional in form although it is based on real
events. Because it is a fictional form you have the same kind of problems that exist in writing a novel, or a play: problems of character-
ization, transition, point of view, etc. I am interested in the relationship between various forms because in many ways I think there are
similarities in the techniques.

I don't think it's possible to make an objective documentary film,
or an objective anything. It's simply one person's version of an aspect
of reality that you've had a chance to photograph, record, think about
and try to structure. No two people can structure that in the same
way; no two people would think about it in exactly the same way. But
the effort in each case is to make a film that is fair to the experience
you had in making the film, to give a fair report on what you have
seen and felt and learned. That frequently is very different from the
point of view that you started out with. I haven't made a film yet in
which I haven't been surprised by the way it comes out.

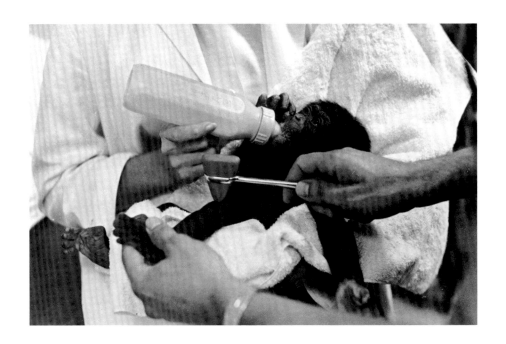

Frederick Wiseman, **Primate**, 1974.

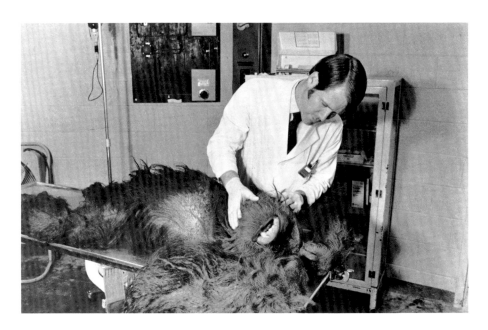

Frederick Wiseman, *A Scientist Examines an Anesthetized Orangutan Prior to Surgery,* **Primate**, 1974.

Frederick Wiseman, *Testing the Effect of Refrigeration,* **Primate**, 1974.

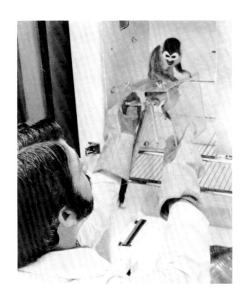

Frederick Wiseman, **Primate**, 1974.

Frederick Wiseman, **Primate**, 1974.

Ultimately, what you're trying to do, what you ask the audience to do when they see the film, is to repeat that process, but clearly with a much smaller amount of material, and to think through their own relationship to what they're seeing and hearing. You're not telling them what their particular response should be to any one sequence. The issue of the audience response is something you really can't have in mind while you're making the film. Once you start thinking about the audience, you have to water down the material to reach the lowest common denominator. At the risk of being arrogant, I always assume that I am the audience. If I didn't do that, I'd be substituting someone else's judgment for my own, and the whole idea of this kind of filmmaking is much too personal to do that.

In a Hollywood film there is usually a one-to-one relationship between a sequence and a point that it's making. In a documentary a scene may be making four or five points at the same time. Take, for example, the sequence in *High School* in which the home economics teacher is instructing the girls about how to be good fashion designers and seamstresses. On the one hand she is totally undercutting them by telling them all that their legs are too thick for the stuff and that there is an appropriate way for women to walk and to dress and that they can't wear certain kinds of clothes if their legs happen to be thicker than those of a Vogue model. Your reaction to that scene is very much dependent on your own values. If you agree with the values of the teacher, then you think she's doing an excellent job. If you think there is something savage about the way she is cutting the girls down and that there is no such thing as a uniform ideal of beauty or attractiveness, then your attitude toward the teacher is very different. That's characteristic of all sequences in documentary films.

You are asking the audience to work in much the same way that you have worked in putting the film together. Frequently there are amazing results. When Louise Day Hicks saw *High School,* for example, she said that she really liked the film, that it had the bittersweet quality of life. You know, I thought that was fine. She happened to be on the other side of all the issues. I didn't really take that as any failure in the point of view of the film because I think that the point of view of the film was quite clear. But her ideology, or values, or whatever you want to call it, was so totally different from mine that she saw the film in a completely different light. That often happens in documentary film when you are trying to make the film reflect the complexity of the reality you're dealing with. The reaction to the film is very much dependent on one's own values.

I've made eight films, and only three of the eight institutions have been unhappy with the results, and then only as a consequence of the reviews. When they first saw the film they always liked it and thought it was fair. They reacted more to the reviews and the way they were characterized in the reviews than they did to the film itself. Except for *Titicut Follies, High School* and *Primate,* the people who gave me permission and who were in the film have generally liked them.

Once the film is made there is the problem of distribution. I did not become involved in distribution to affect social change. I set up my own distributing company six years ago because independent filmmakers are constantly being cheated by film distributors. That's not just paranoia; it happens all the time because the independent filmmaker has no leverage. He may make one film a year or one film

Frederick Wiseman, **High School**, 1968.

Frederick Wiseman. *Dean of Discipline Punishing Student,* **High School,** 1968.

Frederick Wiseman, **Basic Training,** 1971.

every five years and he usually doesn't have the money to send accountants in to check the books or to figure out what's going on, and typically, unless a 16mm film is very successful, once it is turned over to a distributor, you rarely see any money.

After suing a distributor twice, and recovering, I decided that instead of spending money on legal fees, I would rather hire someone who likes the films and is aggressive about getting them distributed on college campuses. The distribution is an enormous amount of work, but if you're not willing to become involved with the business aspects of filmmaking, you're going to be badly taken advantage of. You have to know all about that in order to survive as a filmmaker.

When I first began making films I had a naive view that there was some kind of one-to-one or direct connection between films of this sort and social action or social change. Now I think that was totally naive; there is no connection. In many ways that's probably just as well because if one person were to make a film that would affect ten people, someone else might be able to make a film that would affect ten thousand people in particular ways that you may not like. I don't want to have that kind of power. Ultimately I think it's both presumptuous on the part of the filmmaker and condescending to the audience to think that any work is that powerful. If the films do anything, they provide people with information which they may be in a position to use at some point along the line along with other kinds of information to influence the way they make a decision about something that's going on in society. Then the film becomes one of many experiences that inform that decision. But I do not think that there's any direct connection between a film and a series of change procedures. For example, *Titicut Follies,* which is perhaps the most directly critical film I have done, had little impact on Bridgewater. I had hoped that it would, but it certainly didn't. One indication of that is the trial that took place in the Massachusetts Federal Court in the fall of 1974, seven years after the *Follies* was made. Two inmates brought a suit to close down Bridgewater because of inadequate medical and psychiatric facilities, the lack of which was documented in the film. I have a fairly skeptical view of people who run around, as I once did, with wide eyes saying that they're really going to bring about instant and immediate change.

All the films suggest ideas about how authority is exercised in this society because the theme that unites the films is the relationship of the individual to authority. And in each of the films you see different illustrations of how power is exercised in various institutional settings, and by implication, in other places and other situations. There is a certain similarity between all the films. For example, the things that the Dean of Discipline says in *High School* are almost word for word what the company commander says in *Basic Training.* The difference between the formal and informal attitudes toward authority cuts across all the films and says something, hopefully, not just about the particular place where the film is made but about some larger issues that relate to other places and people.

John
Szarkowski

John Szarkowski was born in Ashland, Wisconsin in 1925 and first began photographing there eight years later. He majored in art history at the University of Wisconsin and while he was a student, worked as a darkroom assistant and photographer in Frederica Cutcheon's portrait studio in Madison. In 1948, he became a staff photographer at the Walker Art Center in Minneapolis, Minnesota. In 1951, he left to become an instructor in photography and art history at the Albright Art School in Buffalo, New York.

Work on his first book, *The Idea of Louis Sullivan,* began in Buffalo with his photographs of the Prudential building. In 1953, he moved to Chicago, home of many of Sullivan's buildings, where he did promotional food advertisements for a commercial studio. In 1954, a Guggenheim Foundation grant allowed him to concentrate his efforts on the completion of his book.

After the publication in 1958 of *The Face of Minnesota,* in which photographs and text were combined to celebrate the state's one-hundredth year, Szarkowski moved to Washburn, Wisconsin and was awarded a second Guggenheim grant to photograph Ontario's Quetico wilderness. In 1962, he became the Director of the Department of Photography at the Museum of Modern Art in New York.

John Szarkowski, *Chicago Auditorium,* 1954.

Evening Lecture

I would like to address myself to what may seem to be a positively primitive question, and consider in an exploratory way the manner in which photography has changed our understanding of the idea of pictorial subject. The fact of the matter, if we are to begin on the basis of full and open disclosure, is that those of us who have thought about photography have not yet made a great deal of progress. Even in terms of historical matters, our knowledge is shot full of ifs and buts, erasures, illegible words, missing chapters, and dubious conjectures. Perhaps we should start back at the beginning and consider the relationship in photography of subject and form.

Photography is a system of picture making in which subject and form are identical and indistinguishable, in which the subject and the picture are beyond argument the same thing. But what interests me most about this would be a corollary which states that the function of the photographer is to decide what his subject is. I mean that this is his *only* function.

The kinds of choices that a photographer makes in the process of defining his subject cover a broad spectrum, ranging from gross choices to exquisitely subtle ones. Beginning on the gross end, the photographer must decide whether he will work in his own backyard or sail off to Egypt or to the moon. Once in Egypt, he has to decide whether to photograph Egyptians or pyramids. From this point on, the decisions become not more important, but subtler: which pyramid? from what vantage point and in what light? in what relation to the picture frame? with what combination of exposure and development in order to achieve a just resolution of the conflicting claims of surface texture, space, volume, and pattern? and then the decisions bearing on the making of a print that will most closely approximate the slippery memory of that true and ephemeral subject that was defined on the site.

The degree of complexity that separates the decisions of Francis Frith from those of Dorothea Lange, photographing a cotton picker in Eloy, Arizona, almost a century later, is obvious enough. But I think

Francis Frith, *The Pyramids of Dahshur*, 1858.

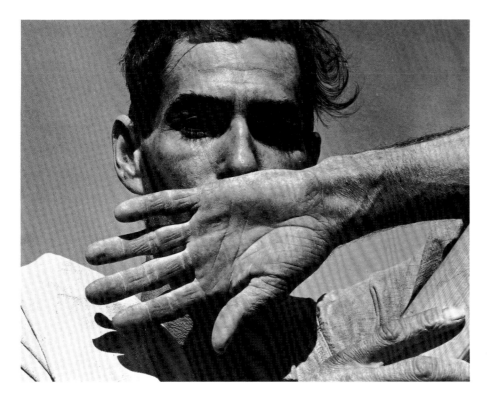

Dorothea Lange, *Migratory Cotton Picker, Elroy, Arizona,* 1940. The Museum of Modern Art, Courtesy of the Library of Congress.

the principle is the same. Choice, intuition, and the winds of chance took Lange to Arizona. By passing a million other potential subjects, she found her way to this particular plantation. There she chose to ignore the landscape, architecture, the beautiful intricate machinery, in order to concentrate on the men who worked there. Among these she chose to photograph a group that included this man. She made several exposures of him and his fellow laborers from a distance as they loaded their cotton. She then decided that she was not yet finished; and she moved closer, homing in on this man, perhaps because he had a good face, more likely, I think, because he was in a good light. By this point, the question of what the subject is involves choices in four dimensions which must be coordinated swiftly and intuitively.

Garry Winogrand, *Dallas,* 1965. The Museum of Modern Art.

If Lange's picture would have been inconceivable to Francis Frith, I think this picture, this subject, by Garry Winogrand would have been almost as startling to Lange. For while her subject might have been at least approximately preconceived in verbal terms, the Winogrand picture depends on the recognition of coherence in the confluence of forms and signs that could not, I think, have been anticipated by the most fertile imagination. This coherence cannot, in fact, be understood in analytical terms while the photographer is working. At this level of complexity, intelligence must become visceral.

The history of photography as a radical picture making system can be defined as the history of the definition of new subjects. Sometimes these new subjects are extensions of ideas that exist in latent form in the work of exceptional photographers of an earlier generation. Sometimes they are genuinely primitive ideas mothered by a new technical breakthrough or a new market demand. But in either case, the picture's new meaning and its new appearance are the same.

I would like now to show you examples from three bodies of work, very different in their motivation and appearance. I'll ask you to judge for yourselves whether or not their content is separable from their aspect. I will show you a group of classical newspaper photographs, some pictures by the great French photographer, Eugène Atget, and some recent photo postcards by a young American photographer named Bill Dane.

News photographs might well be an especially rewarding area for one wishing to study photography in its most basic and unadorned form. Perhaps the reason why this has not been done is that there has been considerable doubt as to whether or not these pictures are really art. If it were possible to avoid this question, I would of course much prefer to, simply because it is not the most interesting or the most useful question. But since it is probably not possible to avoid it, let me answer it quickly and say, "Yes, of course they are art." Not terribly fine art, perhaps, but then fineness is not the only artistic virtue.

Before attempting to define what their subject matter is, we should first clear the air of certain misconceptions by defining what it is not. The subject of news photographs is not news. The simplest way of demonstrating this once and for all would be to persuade a newspaper publisher to reprint, one year after their original appearance, all of the photographs of one year earlier, with slightly varied captions. I don't really think anyone would notice the difference. I do not mean to suggest that newspaper photographs within more or less standardized categories are identical. On the contrary, they are no more identical than the visitations, annunciations, nativities, crucifixions, depositions, resurrections, and assumptions of fifteenth century Italian paintings. News photographs are, however, similar from day to day and year to year, and it is partly in this similarity that their interest lies. A social historian or an anthropologist could surely find much to interest him in the structure and cultural meaning of news photographs, but my own interest is a good deal more modest. I am interested in their character as pictures, by which I mean their iconographic as well as their graphic patterns.

I would like now to suggest several formal characteristics that seem proper to the entire genre and consider them briefly one by one. The pictures are possessed of great narrative ambiguity: without the caption one is never quite sure what is happening. They are hierarchical and formal: what information comes from the picture itself is given within the confines of a rigidly conventionalized technique. They are fragmentary and symbolic: most news photographs are, in one sense or another, close-ups that do not pretend to describe context. They are in large part ceremonial: they deal with events that would not have occurred had they not been newsworthy.

First, these pictures are identified by great narrative ambiguity. Look at this picture and decide for yourself what specific drama is being played out. The young woman on the right is the daughter of the gentleman on the left who has just confessed to murdering his wife, the girl's mother. *Or,* he is the father of the girl's late lover whom she has just shot. *Or,* he is the detective who has just arrested her on the charge of possessing a gun without a license. Or perhaps the gun has nothing to do with the case, but was left there by the policeman who lent his desk to the distinguished family solicitor on the left. Or perhaps the photographer put the gun there to make it a better picture. I apologize for not being able to tell you which, if any, of these stories is true. We did try, but no one seems to remember what the picture was once supposed to have meant. It is a picture that describes the smell and texture of bad trouble and personal tragedy. Its concern is not history, but poetry.

Ed Morgan, **Pittsburgh Sun-Telegraph,** n.d.

These pictures are not natural, but formal. Their true content is determined largely by the photographic and journalistic disciplines that create them; or to put it more simply, their function follows their form. For example, a classic news photograph describes an event that takes place in a flat and shallow space about twelve feet in front of the camera. This plane is determined not, of course, by the objective nature of historical events, but by the preferences of photographers' equipment, the limitations of newspaper reproduction, and the pace at which the photographer works, all of which encourage trust in tried and true formulas.

John J. Reidy, *Murderer Steps into Patrol Wagon*, **New York Daily Mirror,** n.d.

Paul Bernius, *Stephen Baltz, 11, of Willmette, Illinois, lies critically injured on Seventh Avenue, near Sterling Place, Brooklyn. He was the sole survivor in a two plane collision which claimed more than 130 lives in the worst air tragedy in New York City,* **New York Daily News,** 17 December 1960.

Photographer unknown, *Charles Van Doren Winning $104,500 on the T.V. quiz show, "Twenty-One,"* UPI, 21 January 1959.

These pictures are fragmentary and symbolic. Sometimes they are symbolic of genuinely significant events; much more often they symbolize conditions of life that are no more newsworthy than tears. The generic morals of these pictures are generally simple to the point of banality; but the pictures themselves are not banal, for each re-tells the silly old story with a slightly different set of specifics, a different texture of feeling, a different unique face, a new gesture. No two felons cower quite the same; every detective wears his superiority with a slightly different style; the ubiquitous greedy spectator is unendingly fascinating. In the best of these pictures these various signs and symbols come together with perfect economy and surprise to create not merely a catalogue of visual description, but a picture.

Most of these photographs are ceremonial. A good share of them are frankly ceremonial, by which I mean that the ceremony would have occurred in approximately the same form even if photographers had not been there to publicize it, as illustrated by baseball games, prize fights, and courtroom trials. Other kinds of events, once extemporized according to the logical requirements of the event itself, are now planned according to the requirements of photography. Most news is managed news. Generally, however, the news is managed not to conform to a philosophical or a political standard so much as it is managed to conform to the requirements of the techniques by which one reports it. In our literate past, many events, doubtless, were arranged or rearranged so that they might be written about by the poet laureate or the court historian. Today events occur so that they can be photographed.

One of the great charms of early news photographs is that one can't tell which ones are posed and which ones are not. This picture is clearly posed.* The personae have been rearranged to fit more economically within the frame of the picture. Later on it becomes more difficult to tell which pictures are arranged, or at what point in history they are arranged. The sincerity of this picture, to me, is simply beyond challenge. The surprise and delight of the contestant and the sympathetic joy of the TV host at the contestant's miraculously correct answer to the unanswerable $104,500 question are not open to doubt. Even after having been told that Mr. Van Doren's encyclopedic knowledge was assisted by a little judicious prompting, we do not really disbelieve the evidence of the picture. I have been trying to persuade you that the subjects of news photographs are precisely what they appear to be, and that it is only the captions and the editorial page that have made us believe otherwise.

The gulf that separates a photographer like Arthur Fellig, known as Weegee, perhaps the greatest of all news photographers, from a photographer like Eugène Atget, who was perhaps simply the best of all photographers, is a gulf that separates a great natural talent from a profound, original intelligence. Since Atget did not himself write manifestos, it is assumed that he was a talented primitive who wandered aimlessly through Paris, intuitively making wonderful pictures which were beyond his own comprehension. The pictures themselves, some 3000 of which are now in the collection of the Museum of Modern Art, do not support this view. They suggest, on the contrary, a man who understood that photography could be a precise, critical tool, a system with which an artist could define exactly what he thought to be true.

The general and encompassing theme of Atget's work was his own visual life. As an adopted Parisian who loved his city, his visual life was inextricably intertwined with Paris and with his deep appreciation of the fruits of traditional French culture. But he knew the difference between an idea and a sentiment. He knew that while Paris was his arena, his subject was precisely what he defined within the 7 x 9 inches of his little pictures.

---

*Editor's note: Photograph referred to is the *Gloria Trumpeteers,* photographer unknown, Underwood and Underwood, May 8, 1930, in: John Szarkowski, *From the Picture Press.* New York: The Museum of Modern Art, 1973, p. 9.

Atget often made more than one picture of the same subject.* He returned again and again to the trees of St. Cloud and Versailles because he knew that an infinite number of beautiful pictures were potential in them. And he knew also that none of these images was true in the sense that it shared a privileged identity with the object photographed. He did not confuse the subject with the object; he understood that the true subject is defined by the picture. If the tree is the same, the subject is always different.

Atget was concerned with complexity and the relativity of form. The breadth of his interests reminds us of the Encyclopedists of the Enlightenment, but the quality of his sensibility seems prophetically modern. The perspectives of his mind were Copernican rather than Platonic; he worked not from, but toward a formal idea. His conception of form was not nuclear, but galactic, relative, plural, dynamic, provisional, and potential.

Four or five years ago, a young California painter named Bill Dane discovered photography and instantly set out to practice it with enormous enthusiasm and generosity. The generosity expressed itself in the form of a massive barrage of photographic postcards which he sent without obligation and, I suspect, often without acknowledgment, to what would seem to be an enormous mailing list. This is not the manner in which artists have traditionally subsidized their public; so it is perhaps not surprising that when a few critics did begin to take cognizance of Dane's work, they tended to be more interested in the *fact* of the postcards than in the pictures that they carried. But the real reason that I like Dane's postcards is the fact that they have, I think, beautiful pictures on them, pictures that define new subjects. It seems to me that the subject of Bill Dane's pictures is the discovery of lyric beauty in Oakland, or the discovery of surprise and delight in what we had been told was a wasteland of boredom, the discovery of classical measure in the heart of God's own junkyard, the discovery of a kind of optimism, still available at least to the eye.

The trouble and the good part is that these new subjects are defined in visual terms, and no matter how patiently we thumb through our thesauruses, we will not quite reconstruct them with words. The same thing is, of course, true of the news pictures and of those by Atget; but in those cases, at a slightly greater historical remove, it is easier to pay the pictures the compliment of affectionate and knowing gossip. Much of the content of these pictures is concerned, I think, with a kind of visual play, and therefore with agility, surprise, balance, unexpected moves, and grace. The subjects of the pictures are these virtues in themselves, and also the fact that these virtues can flower in such unlikely circumstances. At first acquaintance, the pictures might seem casual. I believe, on the contrary, that their very point and purpose is order. Like much of the best photography being done today, they concern photography's ability to know and rationalize reaches of our visual life that are so subtle, fugitive, and intuitive that until now they have been undefinable and unshareable.

Bill Dane, *Berkeley, California, 27 April 1973*. The Museum of Modern Art.

*Editor's note: For a complete discussion of a series of Atget's trees, which was outlined in more detail in the evening lecture, see: John Szarkowski, "Atget's Trees," *One Hundred Years of Photographic History: Essays in Honor of Beaumont Newhall*, ed. Van Deren Coke. Albuquerque: University of New Mexico Press, 1975, pp. 161-167.

Excerpts from the day seminars

The basic thing I was trying to suggest last night is a very simple idea, which is, fundamentally, that there are not two different ways to say the same thing. You can say *similar* things in two different ways, but you cannot say the same thing.

These two pictures are both by Dorothea Lange. She did the prints; this is not a detail that I pulled out of her pictures or that anybody else pulled out of her pictures. I never want you to think of these two pictures as being the same subject. They're not. They are just the same subject matter in some kind of very vague, amorphous way. Subject matter is raw materials, not the subject. The picture on the right is the full 4 x 5 or 3¼ x 4¼ graflex negative. A good many years later, she decided that she should get in closer and make it more important, and she did the picture on the left. Finally, near the very end of her life, she decided that that was a mistake and went back to the picture on the right. You shouldn't have to know that whatever this building was built as, it was being used as a church. In some sense, you should be able to feel it. The picture itself—what it shows you, the way it describes it to you—should somehow manage to be an equivalent for the sense.

It's always just a photograph. It's describing one's sense of what was there; describing what was there is hopeless, it's impossible. If you begin worrying about that, you're lost. There are a thousand different possibilities, none of which will describe what was there. . . .

When choosing pictures for an exhibition, the photographer and I will overlap eighty per cent on the first try. Fundamentally, it is a matter of trying to trace the way that these individual pictures relate somehow to a common concern and a longer line of how it is possible to use this interesting and funny machine to clarify with some kind of grace the nature of experience. That's the unstated question you're always asking yourself; taste has nothing to do with it. With the other twenty per cent we kind of split the difference, argue about them sometimes until one person or the other is persuaded. When we were doing Dorothea Lange's big retrospective, she was dying. I was not looking forward to the prospect of fighting with her about which pictures, but she made it instantly clear that we were going to fight about it. By and large, most of the time we saw eighty per cent eye to eye, but once in a while she would want to use a picture that seemed to me to be boring. She wanted to use it because of all kinds of irrelevant attachments, and I would say, "No, Dorothea, don't ask me to put that picture in the exhibition. It's not an interesting picture." She would say something like, "Listen to me young man, you were in knee pants and I was there, and that was a very important day. That was the day that men first lined up to get their first social security payments." She would give me a long speech about how important it was, and I would say, "All right, you stand in front of that picture during the twelve weeks of the exhibition and make that speech, blue eyes flashing at everybody who walks through the museum. Then it will be a good picture; otherwise, without the speech, it's not a good picture." You have to really go to the pictures without having read the backs of them first to find out what the difference is between the picture and the caption. . . .

Most of the attempts to use photographs and words together are failures because people try to say the same thing both ways. If you try to do that, you are either relegating the photographs to the func-

Dorothea Lange, *Grayson, San Joaquin Valley, California*, 1938 (cropped version). The Museum of Modern Art.

Dorothea Lange, *Grayson, San Joaquin Valley, California*, 1938 The Museum of Modern Art.

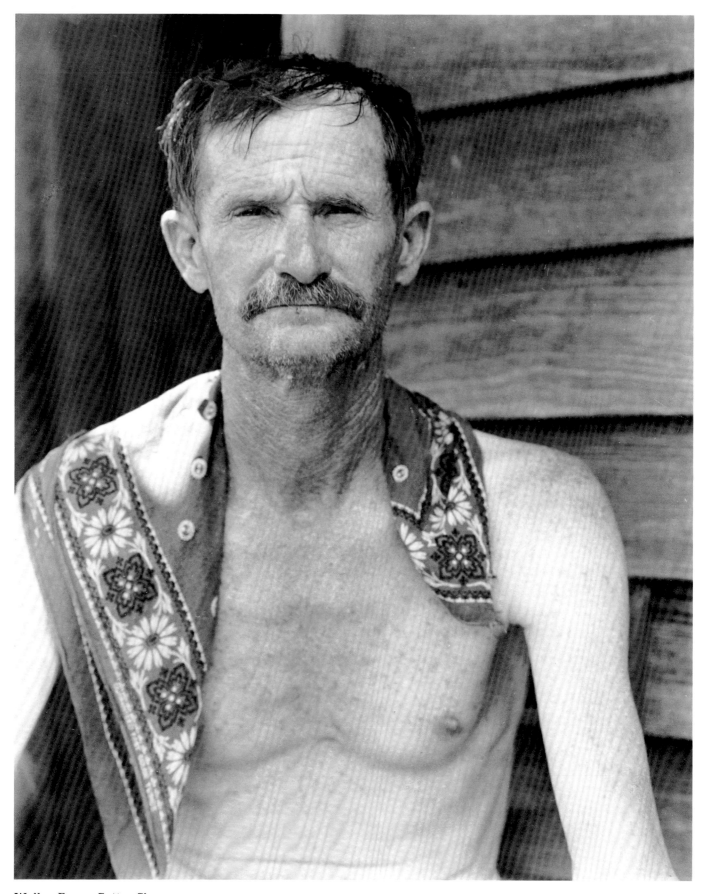

Walker Evans, *Cotton Sharecropper,*
Hale County, Alabama, 1936. The
Museum of Modern Art.

Walker Evans, *Cotton Sharecropper,
Hale County, Alabama,* 1936 (variant
negative). The Museum of Modern Art.

tion of illustrations or you are relegating the words to the function of captions. Either one of these things makes impossible the kind of real collaborative, separate but equal, independent status that the pictures and the text should both have.

The relationship between the pictures and the text is generally brilliant in *An American Exodus* because Lange and Taylor don't try to use the words and the pictures to mean the same thing. Dorothea was a marvelous writer. She wrote very well, and very carefully. And she did very good field notes. I suspect that she worked them over too, after she got home. Paul Taylor was a proper, trained social scientist and believed you wrote down all the facts right then, before you forgot them. He was doubtless a very good influence on Dorothea in that respect. . . .

A lot of you know this picture on the left from *Let Us Now Praise Famous Men* or from other Walker Evans sources. Very few people know that this man had a twin brother, a nicer fellow, not so intelligent, but sweeter. I love to look at these two photographs as an example of how fine you can slice it and what a difference it can make. Which is the better picture? [Student response: "The one on the left."] Sure it is. The next thing you would ask is "Why are the two men different? Why are they different subjects?" You ask yourself technical questions just like any other kind of art historian. You ask "What's the difference?" and the difference is the flash fill. Evans used a flashbulb for the one on the right, and you see into those eyes. They don't become those opaque, really frighteningly anonymous little black slits. The whole quality of the rendering of his face is softened by that flash filling in those shadows, smoothing the contours of his face. Also with the flash you stop down a little bit, so the rendering of the background is different; the boards behind are a little sharper, the ears are sharper. You can go through and make a long list of what physically are the differences between these two.

I don't mean to suggest that what these two pictures share is not more important than their differences. What these two subjects have in common is, of course, more important than the very subtle differences between them. My guess would be that if there had been some kind of disaster on the negative on the left, it's perfectly possible, I think probable, that Walker still would have liked the picture on the right enough to use it. Photographers are always dealing, if they're really good, with circumstances that are only barely and marginally under control. If you're only going to make photographs that you can *absolutely* and precisely predict, if you can *really* absolutely previsualize it, why make it?

People who are not photographers do not realize how fast and irretrievably things change, even in tiny subtle ways. What Ansel Adams is dealing with is just as ephemeral as what Cartier-Bresson was dealing with, or what Garry Winogrand is doing. And it doesn't have to be the waves splashing on the surf; it can just be the quality of the light. . . .

Of the kind of hard-core modern twenties artists who worked in photography, I think Moholy, in many ways, has a lot more juice in him now to be made use of than most of the others. There is something in Moholy which is very usable. It has to do with a terrific sense of openness toward the machinery, toward the medium, and almost a great pleasure in what the camera could do that he didn't completely understand. He welcomed it, he courted it—the wonderful

Lázló Moholy-Nagy, *Spring, Berlin,*
1928. The Museum of Modern Art.

kinds of little visual jokes, ambiguities, surprises that are in his pictures that, on one level, he managed to make clear.

For ten years I thought that man was in the tree, and then for about five years I thought that no, he was not in the tree, he was on the ground. It turns out he is in the tree. The picture has got to do with something that certainly Moholy was not totally and absolutely in all of its aspects conscious of when he made it. It's an exploration; it's enormously complicated, as most photographs are. There's an awful lot going on. You try to keep all of the oranges in the air as best you can, and once in a while it works. Then you've got a good one, and that improves the sensitization of your reactions. There's a quality of confrontation in Moholy's pictures, the presence of a problem that hasn't absolutely been solved to death. A lot of photographs about which one can say absolutely nothing bad are still just not interesting pictures because there was never any risk. You feel that the photographer had the solutions, but he had no problem. . . .

In terms of what they feel is of use to them, the good artists have a very strong, not necessarily objective, sense of just exactly what has been done and where the end of the diving board is, today, right now, this morning. It's the hobbyist, then, who keeps coming in with bad, third-rate imitations of things people did marvelously well in the

twenties, thinking that he has done something original. I think that
one of the things that characterizes the attitudes of people who seem
to me to be bright and open, sophisticated young photographers is
their much more catholic interest in the tradition. They are looking
at a much wider range of kinds of pictures and are much less concerned with whether or not the picture, on the surface of it, is clearly
and unmistakably identifiable as art....

Part of what I've been trying to talk about probably derives from
a long series of my own misunderstandings over the course of many
years of being interested in photography. I first saw this picture when
I was a little kid. It was titled, *End of an Era,* and there was no doubt
in my mind whatsoever about what the subject matter of that photograph was—who that woman was in her chauffeur-driven elegant
automobile looking down at the pedestrian through that beautiful
round window, with the hand protecting her nose from any possible
offense from the street. I thought that was marvelous, the way that
photographer had pinned her to the specimen board like a moth. I
kept on thinking that was the subject of the photograph until thirty
or so years later, when I was working with Lange on her exhibition.
For the very first time in my life I found a full caption to the picture. It
was *End of an Era, Funeral Cortege in a Small Valley Town,* and my
philosophical sense of what the content of the picture was was absolutely totally destroyed, instantly. The picture didn't change, and
my love of the picture and my pleasure in the picture didn't change;

Dorothea Lange, *Funeral Cortege, End
of an Era in a Small Valley Town,
California,* 1938. The Museum of
Modern Art.

Henri Cartier-Bresson, *Children Playing in Ruins, Seville,* 1933. The Museum of Modern Art.

I didn't have to abandon the picture because it meant something different—it was now grief I was looking at instead of some other emotion. It was an interesting lesson.

I have a whole string of those misconceptions. For years I thought that all those Cartier-Bresson pictures of the children playing in the ruins in Seville were from the Spanish War: children playing in the midst of this cruelly bombed-out city. I was a photographer in those days, not a curator, and I didn't have to look closely at the dates. But those pictures were done four years before the war started. It finally sank through my head that if I wanted to fasten some kind of larger social, political, philosophical record to them, it would have to be something other than the war or fascism or the United Front because the pictures were four years premature. But they haven't changed either. . . .

I don't think complete ignorance is possible; I don't even think it's advisable. If we weren't willing and interested in trying, attempting to deal with the pictures intellectually, there would be no point in talking about them because that's fundamentally the only way we can try to deal with them—in words, by talking about them. And I don't in any way mean to suggest that these are purely abstract constructions that have their meaning enclosed completely within their frame and do not reverberate outside in the rest of the whole world of our knowledge and our sensibility. How boring that would be, how terribly dry and limited. But it is important to make the distinction between what is inside the picture and what is outside the picture. Then we can allow the photograph to release and enliven our knowledge or memory or sensibility so that we can make different kinds of connections with what we already know and what we didn't know until we looked at the picture, in terms of what is in the picture.

I think what a good picture does is demand your attention. That doesn't mean every good picture is going to stop you on the street like the Ancient Mariner. Sometimes you have to be a little more open to it, and it takes a little more time for it to persuade you that it's a really good picture; but once it persuades you, what it wins by that is your attention. You try to bring as much of yourself to it as you can. In the

Dorothea Lange, *Migrant Mother, Nipomo, California,* 1936. The Museum of Modern Art.

Diana Thorne, *Spanish Mother, The Terror of 1938,* lithograph, 1939. The Museum of Modern Art.

course of a lifetime you might make up a hundred different stories about the same picture, all of which are indefensible but each of which is a kind of compliment.

One could do very interesting research about all of the ways that the *Migrant Mother* has been used; all of the ways that it has been doctored, painted over, made to look Spanish and Russian; and all the things it has been used to prove. It's interesting because the picture is almost totally ambiguous. If one tried to define precisely what that photograph documents, one could not locate it in any given decade, one could not with any confidence describe the condition of this woman and her family as being desperately poor. Certainly one of the terribly interesting things about pictures is that they do attract to themselves wonderful rich bodies of speculation and superstition and fairy tale that, for better or worse, are part of what we're going to do to things that interest us.

W. Eugene Smith

Born in 1918, in Wichita, Kansas, Smith's early interest in photographing airplanes led to work for local newspapers during his high school years. In 1936 he entered the University of Notre Dame on a unique photography scholarship; he left for New York after one semester. After a brief stay with *Newsweek* Smith joined the staff of *Life* in 1939. Discontented with his assignments and with *Life*'s shallow treatment of its material, Smith resigned in 1941. Interest in World War II ended his freelance activity and after some wartime experience on special assignments for various publications he rejoined *Life*'s staff in 1944 as a war correspondent in the Pacific. Badly wounded in 1945 on Okinawa while working on a story, he returned to New York. "The Walk to Paradise Garden," a picture of his two children, marked the end of two years of forced inactivity during convalescence. A rich period of work for *Life* followed, to be ended by a dispute over the handling of "A Man of Mercy," an article on Albert Schweitzer. This dispute resulted in Smith's resignation in 1954. He joined Magnum Photos, and received two Guggenheim Fellowships while working on an essay begun in 1955 on the city of Pittsburgh. Various independent projects, teaching positions, and preparation of a book meant to encompass his life's work entitled *The Walk to Paradise Garden* occupied his time during this period of general recognition. In 1961 he began working in Japan. In 1963 he was appointed to the President's Committee on Photography. He was awarded a third Guggenheim Fellowship in 1969. Smith married again in 1971 and with his wife, Aileen, began three and a half years of work in Minamata, which was interrupted in early 1972 when he was badly beaten up while photographing. The book, *Minamata,* appeared in 1975.

New York, 1971.

I started when I was fourteen. I wanted to be an aircraft designer. I took up photography so that I could photograph the planes that were coming through Wichita, Kansas, where I was born. Within about six weeks I was publishing pictures in the local newspaper. And then I became much more interested in photography than in the designing of planes. In that way I was very lucky because I never had to design a war plane, which made me feel rather good.

The first things that I photographed were mostly in two categories: one was sports; and the other was the dust bowl, dust storms, and drought. I've always credited the photographing of sports as giving me a head start in the matter of the reflex timing that is needed in most photography. I still like to photograph sports, or I like to photograph out of a train window or a car window, just to keep my reflexes working at high tension. I learned to photograph this way until quite a few pictures seemed to me just about as well composed as any other pictures of mine. This development of a strong sense of timing has been very helpful in almost any kind of participatory photography that I have done. The other, the dust bowl photography, as people called it, matured me very early in life. I was really photographing the destruction of my own family as well as the destruction of an entire area. I had the right in school to get up and leave any class at any time and go out and photograph. All I had to do was just excuse myself, but with the promised condition that I kept my grades up. I would see a dust storm coming up and I would say "excuse me." This was when I was fourteen, fifteen, sixteen.

Then when I was seventeen the University of Notre Dame created a photographic scholarship for me. I'm afraid I only lasted one

97 W. EUGENE SMITH

semester, leaving on Washington's birthday. I wouldn't have left Notre Dame, probably, but for the fact that I flunked history. I mean, according to the teacher. And since history was my strong subject, I didn't quite understand how I had flunked it. I had gone in, looked at the questions, sat down, and I wrote for three hours, I think. I got it back and it said sixty-six. And I asked the teacher, "Is there some mistake?" I just couldn't see how I could have gotten such a low grade. I never got such a tongue-lashing in my life, daring to question the teacher. So I walked right out of the history class. I was so furious, and I wanted to leave anyway. I walked over to the Western Union office and sent my mother a wire and told her I was going to New York. When I got to New York, I got a letter from my roommate saying, "Ha, ha. You were right and he was wrong. You had a ninety-six." Such small things can change the course of a life. I went to work for *Newsweek* and was fired for using a small camera—a 2¼ x 2¼, not a 35. Well, they were very old fashioned at the time. They wanted a Speed Graphic camera, not a small 2¼ x 2¼. They were afraid of it, I think. They forbade me to use a small camera on an assignment, any assignment. I like the big camera; I like the small camera. But, I decided that the small camera was much better suited to the job. And so I photographed with a small camera. Without even looking at the pictures, they said, "What camera did you use?" And it was lucky, too, that they fired me, because then I started working for *Life*.

There are many stories as to why *Life* folded. One was that they were losing so much money. My personal opinion is that *Life* would not have had to fold if they had edited differently. In other words, I'm still carrying on the same battle with them that I've carried on all through the years. In the early fifties I used to tell them, "I just don't see how you can continue to live, unless you change your attitude of editing and unless you can do more stories that have the depth and the compelling power to gain your readers and really hold them." And frankly, my stories were among the most successful that *Life* ever used. I had to fight for all of them to get publication. If they had just treated many other subjects with greater depth and greater feeling—instead of, in the end, considerable superficiality—I think they would have survived.

I have a letter from *Life* which said something about "your friends here at *Life* have decided you either cannot or will not be saved." When *Life* folded I was in Tokyo and was told about it on the platform of a subway station. I felt very badly about it, but that sentence crossed my mind because when I had said to *Life,* "I don't see how you can continue to live," I never expected them to go out of business. It was not really a question; I really believed they were unshakable.

As to my photography of human beings, compared to *Life*'s usual approach, it is a lot harder to do it my way. I just simply wanted to give the time and the effort to take the superficiality out of a story. After I did, *Life* often would bring back that superficiality.

They came up with many fresh ideas, but too often they treated a fresh idea in the same old way. Too often, especially in the earlier days, they would issue scripts including what photographs should be made. These would be written by generally inexperienced individuals in the main office, perhaps 1,500 or 2,000 miles away from the individuals in the story. If a script said a farmer in South Dakota went to his outhouse every morning at 3:00 am—even though he had the most modern of toilets—the photographs very likely would show him going to his neighbor's outhouse. I just, well, read the script and threw it away. It was a hell of a way to run a magazine "of reality."

My attitude almost always was friendly towards *Life;* in spite of their faults and failures they were a great magazine; otherwise it would not have been worth the fight. The resignation over the Schweitzer essay—it was a battle over the right of responsibility for my reportage, I was bluntly saying they could not run a story of mine and distort it, and I resigned trying to force them to work out the problems about the story.

I would have gone back to work with *Life* at any time if they had written into my contract a "right of responsibility" clause including the right to prevent publication of any story that was being distorted from my reportage; but *Life* became fearful that if they gave a right like that to one person they would have to give it to all. Which might have been a good idea, but it wasn't true, because very few of the others were willing to work that hard or to fight like that over how their pictures were used.

I really felt very alone at times, and still do. As I have said, there were very few who were trying to do what I was trying to do—they generally were not that troublesome, even though some did resign for one reason or another. Most of the stories of my being temperamental came from these battles—but as far as I am concerned, I am responsible for everything that goes in, as far as having the responsibility that it should not be distorted. In their setup I was not responsible in the sense that it was "not my job" to handle words, but I wanted those words to be quite great and I tried very hard to make sure they were.

If I was going to be so temperamental as to turn down stories all the time, I had to bring in something that was equivalent, that would be at least as satisfactory. And this was the only way I could insure that I would work on stories *I* wanted to work on. As to your question about the "Nurse Midwife"—they more or less went right ahead and said, "Fine, go up and talk to the science department." The science department and I got along very well. I had great respect for the people there, and we worked together like intelligent people, without any of the pettiness that went on in so many other departments. Well, the reason I thought they were intelligent is that they mostly left me alone. No, they were very good, marvelous at their job, too. I said, "too," I shouldn't have said that. I was in on most of the layouts, especially toward the end of our togetherness. It isn't necessary, in my mind, for me to do every layout. Actually, in those days at *Life,* they could change my layout, as long as it did not insult my intelligence, and as long as it did not distort the meaning of the story. I did not throw temperamental tantrums about such things. I've never thrown a temperamental tantrum in my life, anyway. As far as I'm concerned, my temperament was backed into by having this happen and that happen; that just made me determined that such a thing would not happen the next time. So it was not that I was trying to throw weight around. In fact, I think I'm very easy to get along with in such matters, as long as there are intelligent and sincere people equally trying to do a job. I don't really think there's much reason just to go around being temperamental. I think it gets in the way of doing a job well. So all the resignations, etc., were for purposes of trying to help me gain the quality in the magazine I felt was my responsibility as a

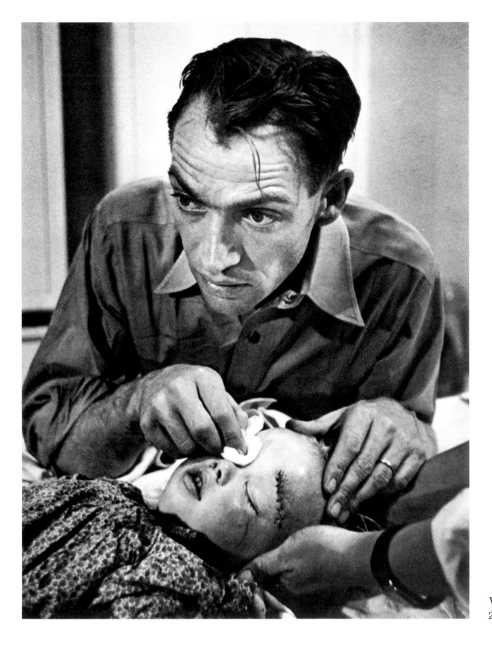

W. Eugene Smith, *Country Doctor,* **Life,**
20 September 1948.

journalist. And I take that responsibility very seriously. Although we laugh at some of the escapades, as you might call them, or scenes that took place, they were all very serious and never light.

I don't think there is anything that has replaced *Life.* Certainly television has not. And I think we are less well off than we were when it was alive. I think it's too bad, because I think through television we remain with the delusion that we are among the most informed people in the world, and informed much faster; and I think we are rapidly approaching a state of being very *uninformed.* This constant, instant journalism—you don't get much journalism with it; you don't get much depth. I'm utterly unsatisfied with news broadcasts. However, our pictures appeared very frequently in Japan, and they appeared very often on prime time television; I cannot see that happening here very much. The Japanese use still photographs on their television shows much more intelligently than we do. I've had several half-hour and hour-long programs, or Aileen and I have, and this is how we influence. The ways of seeing here and the use of still photographs are not very intelligent as yet. Television is doing the same thing that *Life* did, as far as that goes, in most of their hour-long specials. I have to give them the same warning: if they don't do better, it's just not going to work.

Well, I threatened resignation many times. I only had three powers. One was to suggest; another was to protest; and the third was to threaten resignation. And one has to be fairly confident in oneself to threaten it, and it can never be a bluff. So actually I resigned for the first time in 1940. The reason was that the assignments were just simply poor assignments, and I wanted to do something much more serious. So I wrote a letter saying this to the photographic editor and he wrote back saying he, too, once wanted to write "the great American novel." So I resigned at that time. And he said I would never have another chance to work for *Life* magazine. I mean, they couldn't just let a young guy resign; they had to put a threat, a twist, into it. So when the war came, and later when they wanted me back, I made them ask me five times. No, seriously, it wasn't just vengeance. It was the fact that I did not like the attitude that *Life* used to have of trying to keep people scared and in this way, to get more mileage out of them as a photographer or a writer. I felt that if they really had to work to get me back, I would be in a much better position to stand them off.

Wilson Hicks made some remark that I re-posed pictures in a way that was more real than reality itself. Don't take any of the words in Wilson's book about me as accurate. He also takes credit for my going to the Spanish village, and he had already been off the staff. He's the one that instituted the statement that if we could just break the idealism of Smith, we could get more mileage out of him as a photographer. After our fairly early battles, and after he found out he couldn't do all this pushing around, he and I got along fairly well. I knew where he stood and he knew where I stood. The "Country Doctor" was during this period of breaking the idealism out of Smith, and I was beaten down in some ways. I was going to resign when I came back. I didn't; things had changed. To do the "Country Doctor" I had to sneak out of town because I was getting no assignment that was in any way compatible with me at that moment, because they were either refusing to give me any assignment that was workable, or I was not working at all. Hicks and his assistants were on vacation. The suggestion for the "Country Doctor" was not my suggestion, it was *Life's*. But, I was determined, really, I was going to do this absolutely my way or that was the end. We started doing it, and Hicks started sending wires that I should come back. Finally, I sent a wire back to each one of his which said: "Sorry, to leave now would jeopardize the story." Incidentally, the "Country Doctor" story took twenty-three days and twenty-three nights; and it also is the story that did more than any other to break *Life*'s habit of issuing scripts for every story. Finally, Hicks stopped outside my door one day and said, "I hear you've got a very good story in there." And I said, "Well, it's not too bad." And then he said, "I doubt if you can guess who told me." And I thought, "Well, why did he ask me a question like that?" Hicks' attitude of playing people off against people, of playing one man against another, of making someone work out of fear instead of real cooperation, is why I resigned from *Life* to begin with—I mean, one of the reasons that I had—because I could not work under those kinds of conditions. I thought, "Well, who did he most want me to start a feud with or something. Who is he playing off against me?" I took a chance and said, "Leonard McCombe." I was right. And this

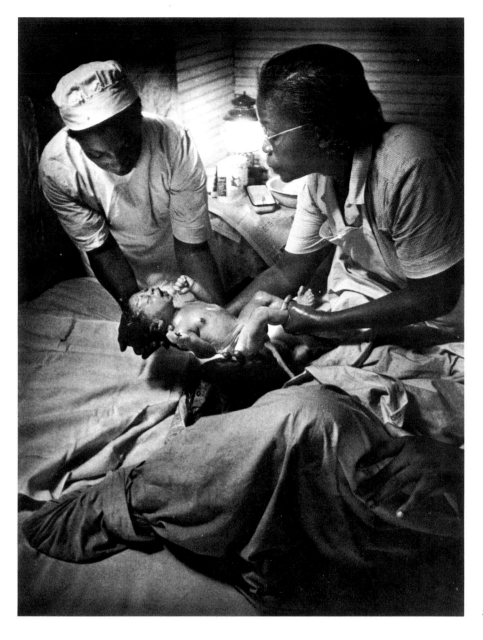

W. Eugene Smith, *Nurse Midwife,* **Life,**
3 December 1951.

was because Leonard McCombe had just done his very famous
"Career Girl." I think Wilson got Leonard and me mixed up as to who
was setting up pictures. It never interfered with Leonard's and my
friendship.

I almost *never* pose a picture. There was one time when I was
about nineteen or twenty that I did everything in a posed way with
many, many flashbulbs. I once decided that was the wrong way and
I tore them all up. Now I wish I hadn't. There is one thing that I will
do. Many people say that if you tamper with your subject at all or use
any additional lights that this is not honest. Well, I don't think that
light has anything to do with honesty. For instance, doing the "Midwife" the rooms were frequently smaller than this table and much
shorter, and if I was trying to relate the midwife to the woman who
was giving birth, I had to somehow have pictures that showed both.
Sometimes I could use a window, but I would not hesitate at all to
go in a few days before the child was expected and, say, even move
the bed just far enough away from the wall so I could photograph
across the expectant mother and show the midwife. And also, since
most of the rooms were very dark, I very likely would carry a white

card and possibly bounce strobe from it. Now this, some people say, is interfering with your subject. But that in no way is interfering with the natural fact and actual fact of the childbirth. So I never hesitated to do it. There was a school of "available light photography" that I think was rather a nonsensical school, in that they said that the honesty of photography was dependent upon just using the light that was available. I think if people are honest enough in the way they approach their subjects, they do not need some school of approach that is a mechanical limitation. My attitude toward available light is: any damned light is available light if I can get my hands on it when I need it. And I have used a match, for instance, to get just the touch of light into a face, or a hand flashlight. I almost never light the subject, but I'm saying these are devices I will use if I think it is necessary. Light is not necessarily honest; human beings may be.

I, unlike some photographers, when I'm photographing, will *never* get so carried away—I may be crying and it's hard to photograph through tears, in some situations, some of the pictures in Minamata and other places—but I never lose track of what I am doing. I keep a clear mind as to what I am doing. Many photographers, good ones, Bourke-White and Wayne Miller, have both said that very often when they are in a dramatic situation they get so carried away taking photographs that they don't really realize anything else that is going on or what they really have until they see their photographs. This is a perfectly legitimate way to work. I sometimes wonder if maybe I don't get carried far enough away. For instance, take the picture of the mother and the child from the Minamata series. I had built up to a very high tension. I turned to Aileen and I said, "Well, okay, I have the photograph," and from that exposure on I got sloppy in my focus and sloppy in my lighting. And so, actually what I was doing was trying to keep enough tension going so that if anything else developed, I would be prepared to come to full tension again. As it was in that photograph, I usually know what is happening unless I'm being fairly mediocre. And if I'm being fairly mediocre, then, of course, there are ten mediocre photographs I can't choose from.

As we photographed other things, things around her, and even the family, it grew and grew in my mind that to me the symbol of Minamata was, finally, a picture of this woman and the child, Tomoko. One day I simply said to Aileen that if everything is all right up there, and they are not too busy, let us try and make that symbolic picture. Now this does not in any way mean I was posing the picture in the sense of posing a picture. It meant that I was interpreting what by now I knew full well to be true, because I would never have done it otherwise. And so we went there and we sat; and we talked for a while; and, I actually explained what kind of a picture—I didn't explain that I wanted that look, that look of courage—I simply said that I wanted something of the caring for Tomoko. I thought maybe away from the bath would be the picture that would best show what had happened to Tomoko's body. We started. The mother herself suggested that the photograph should be in the bath; so we decided to try that. The mother went through her ordinary bath routine with the child, and this was the result.

I very often do this where I realize that that kind of a picture is legitimate to an essay; I simply sharpen my perception watching for that event to happen. And I wouldn't hesitate, say, to set a legitimate situation into motion if I thoroughly felt that the picture was legiti-

W. Eugene Smith, *Tomoka and Mother,*
Minamata, 1972.

mate to the subject. I almost never do this, but I wouldn't hesitate to do it if there were an important gap in the coverage of the event. I much prefer to wait for the event to happen in natural life than to speed it up.

Except when covering the war, I find that my approaches are not very different. I generally try to become so accepted into a community, that they more or less forget about me as a photographer and as a journalist, and I will be welcomed in homes and not as a stranger intruding. Part of this is also that I'm so very shy that I do not feel I can just go out and slam cameras in people's faces and photograph them. I never could do some of the things that some of the people, who I think are very fine photographers, do. I'm not saying I'm right and they're wrong. I'm just saying that it's just not my way of working. So the "Midwife" and *Minamata* were, in a sense, approached in the same way; although *Minamata* did have much more of the confrontations between patients and company, and one of its results was their smashing my head and my camera. When we speak of that situation, it only took thirty seconds of my life, as far as the action that caused it to happen. And though I'm still suffering from it, I would like to balance that action with the good things and the warmth with which most of the Japanese people have treated me. The Japanese acceptance of me has just been remarkable.

When you go to a city or village like Minamata, the great, the most grievous problem as far as I am concerned is how to reach the patients. How do you get them to accept you so that you can photograph? The question of photographing them is a question of intrusion; it is a question of depth; it is a question of learning your subject well enough to know how to photograph. I thoroughly believe that in all photography this is *most* important. I don't believe one should intrude when the intrusion is obnoxious, or dangerous, or it just truly is within the rights of the subject to object. I have complete sympathy for anyone who does object. Becoming closely enough acquainted with the subjects is a question that no one can tell you how to solve, but it is a question of how to be intimate enough so that they forget that you are a photographer to the extent that they will not be self-conscious when you are around. And in Minamata it reached that point in three or four months with most of the neighbors, most of the people, accepting me.

I truly at all times try to have consideration for the people I'm photographing. I try to become as intimate with the subjects as possible. For instance, with the "Midwife," I felt it didn't matter whether I took one camera or five because the shock of *their* seeing a white man with any kind of a camera coming across toward their shack was traumatic. Yet because they had such a reverence or love for the midwife, all she would have to do to get them at their ease would be to say, "This is Mr. Smith. He's a friend of mine. We are working together." That usually just ended all embarrassment; it ended all hesitation, although there were always certain kinds of shyness and there always will be. There are many ways lives can be changed by photographs, but I don't think just the mere act of making a photograph will cause it to change.

In the death scene in the "Spanish Village," I did not want to intrude into the mourning scene. But as the picture came about, the day before I had been quite ill with an upset stomach in the field just on the edge of the village. A man offered me some wine, which I didn't want, but I drank it anyway just because of the gesture of kindness. Then the next day he came to me and said his father had died that night. He had had gangrene and they wanted to bury him as quickly as possible, so he asked me if I could take him to the county seat so he could get the necessary papers registered. When we came back, he went to his house. I could see into the house; it was a very moving scene that was happening in the back of the room, but I could not bring myself to go in, to just walk in; I just couldn't do it. I paced back and forth outside, storming at myself because I realized that it was an important picture, and it was important to the whole story. But yet I did not feel I had the right to intrude. And I knew that a great many photographers would have just gone in. Whether they would have come out with a good picture, I don't know, because they probably would have disturbed the people in there. Well, I stayed outside for a while. Then I saw the son of the man come to the door, and I suddenly went up to him and said, "Sir, I do not wish to dishonor your father, but would it be permissable for me to enter your house and to photograph?" And he said, "Please come in. I would be honored." So I went in with one assistant. The only light in there was a candle about three feet over his head, and with all that black that they were wearing, it was *very* difficult. But I wanted to hold that same mood of lighting, so it was one of the few times I used a flashbulb. I took the reflector off and just used the bare bulb. By hand signals alone I motioned my assistant to work his way around behind the people to a position where he could hold the bulb over the candle so that it would simulate the candle lighting. I made one exposure and immediately realized that it was not good, that the picture was all out of rhythm. I made one more and I thought I had at least a good picture. I would have loved to have stayed there and photographed for a couple of rolls, but then I saw the son standing in the doorway peering in. I again motioned without words for my assistant to go through the other doorway so that mourners in the other room and the son in the doorway could be seen, made one more exposure, and then very reluctantly I left. All this time never having said a word, hoping I never created much of a disturbance. So I think a great many of these very delicate

W. Eugene Smith, *Spanish Village,*
Life, 9 April 1951.

situations can be overcome with care and sensitivity and politeness. I have known other instances where I absolutely have refused to photograph, though, because I think there is no photograph that is worth any real embarrassment to the people involved.

Actually, I think my whole career has followed this involvement with individuals and situations that are very much part of what I am today. My aims have been pretty much the same. There have been curves and jags, but it's still an unbroken line from where I began to where I am now. I think for a long while I was getting better. In the early fifties, I think I was going so rapidly from each story I was attempting that it could have been remarkable to keep up that growth. Then came a very bad period in my life, but I was still growing for several years within it. I think I was at my peak as a photographer in, say, 1958, or so. I do not think that I am as good a photographer today as I was then. My imagination and my seeing were wildly free and disciplined. Everywhere I looked, every time I thought, it seemed to me it left me with greater exuberance and a truer quality for seeing. Yet, it was one of the most miserable times of my life for I had little opportunity to put it into real use. I only had small opportunities to do it, but I can still feel it happening. Actually, I also wrote more in that time. I think my writing was better then, too, than it is now—I wrote two plays. I could not write them today.

I'm a great believer in life. Oh, my sense of despair is one of sorrows and deep feelings, but it is not one of giving up on either the world or other people. The world or other people, now what does that mean? I sometimes give up in despair on my English, but not on people. No, I think I'm one of the most affirmative photographers. There's nothing in this essay *[Minamata]* that can be taken as being other than affirmative, no matter how cynical I am at times and no matter how critical I am at other times. The basic feeling is affirmation; it is not despair. And I really mean that.

I've been very lucky. I started when I was fourteen and in terms of acceptance, I've been a success almost the entire time. In fact, I've had to keep tight control to make sure that my self-criticism never got dulled by good notices or I could easily have slipped into real complacency. I compete only against myself—what do you think that was a minute ago when I said I was a better photographer in 1958? Was the criticism plain? I think *Minamata* should have been better. I've never been satisfied with the work I've done. My work is a failure as far as the height I'd like to reach with it. You see, I started out on the premise that there's no such thing as a perfectionist. Because knowing perfection is impossible, the perfectionist never begins. So knowing that I'm going to fail to a certain extent, my problem is to cut that failure down to as narrow a gap as possible.

By far the best way to see Minamata is by means of the book that is just coming out, because I think we have tried to blend words and pictures together in a way that they really don't repeat each other. Each adds to the other medium in a true marriage. A few of the captions do slightly repeat, but all in all, I don't think they do. Now I have not laid it out as a photographer trying to look good as a photographer as such. I mean, in other words, this is an essay which I hope becomes an experience for those who read it. I'm not trying to say: "Oh, see what a great photographer I am," or something like that. Sometimes I have used pictures, pictures that I simply had not been able to bring to the very highest of photographic standards, but that

I found to be essential for the book. Ideally every photograph would fill both the artistic function and the necessity of journalism.

I put so much passion and so much energy into the doing of my photographs that beyond photography for art's sake, "art for art's sake," or such, I much prefer to have my photographs add this other element, that possibly they will stir someone to action, to do something about something. I would like to make clear at the very beginning that I have no conflict between journalism and my artist self. At one time I did, but then I realized that to be a good journalist I needed to be the finest artist that I could possibly be. When I was working for *Colliers,* I really rather enjoyed reading a manuscript and then illustrating the manuscript in some way, some very free-form way that allowed me not to illustrate one little passage or something, but allowed me to illustrate the feeling of the subject. I think it's generally easier to do the words after the pictures, because in a way you have more flexibility with words than you do with a photograph.

I learned much more from music, literature, the stage, the other arts, than I ever learned from painting or from photography. I don't know why that should be. I picked up timing and a sense of drama, and also how to relate pictures together. But more important than that, I was also emotionally very deeply stirred; my mind was set to thinking; I was just involved. My music was of the widest possible variety. So was my outlook on life as far as what it embraces. I have about twenty-five thousand records and ten thousand books. I've lived a little bit of life, too. Drama plays a great role in my photography. You very seldom will find among my photographs someone who is standing there, just staring at me. I like very much to have my portraits in relationships, so that the person you are looking at is well related to a background of some of the things that he has. And I try to integrate these very strongly into the final photograph.

I was a terrible printer; in fact, some people think I still am. My printing style mainly evolved from an effort to defeat printers. I would work very hard so that anything that was essential to the picture would be very open and easy to see, and shadowed details would be open. So it would have a chance, even if it didn't come out as good printing, it would at least bear a resemblance to the balances that I was working toward.

I think that color—in the form that it is in now, and in the lack of control that I would have over it—has a great tendency to vulgarize the kinds of emotions that I'm trying to express. Now, color should not vulgarize emotions because it should be a marvelous tool for underlining them and intensifying them, but I just cannot stand most of the color I see, especially in reproduction.

The photographer who influenced me possibly the most when I was very young was a man by the name of Martin Munkacsi. I don't know of anyone who has, as a photographer, influenced me most, but it was his sense of humanity and dynamics that most impressed me, his almost poster-like quality whether he was photographing the Nazis goose stepping or the unguarded moments of high officials. But I can't say too many photographers have influenced me. There are those I admire, and I absorb from all sources, obviously. Now Robert Frank, I have to relate him to Franz Kafka. I just feel an unatoned thinking within Bob that I do relate to, and I like his pictures for that reason. He's going to make them anyway, so whatever I think about his sensitivity is not going to injure anyone. I feel worried about

Diane Arbus' pictures, what they have done to the subject, but I also admire her as a photographer. Although with Diane Arbus I've often wondered if, quite independently of each other, we had both accidentally run across the same people and had photographed them—not being influenced by knowing that the other person was influencing us—I really would have loved to have seen the difference the photographs would show. Some of her people I think I would perhaps have chosen as subjects, too, but I think they would have come out vastly different. Now, I don't think either one of us would necessarily be right, but I think we would have shown vastly different interpretations of the same people. And I think a lot of her freaks would not look so freaky, and in fact, I think they would look quite normal.

As far as I am concerned, I just very quietly accept photography as an art. Some of the photographs I've taken have changed others' lives, too, because I know from the history of my own work that at times through photographs I have been able to destroy a concentration camp; I have been able to build a clinic for a nurse midwife; I have in some measure been able to help a little fighting the disease and pollution of racism. I never knew quite the answer when individuals asked me my reason for becoming involved in pollution. And then I suddenly realized that in my entire life I have seldom been seriously photographically involved with anything else. I grew into a quick maturity seeing my own family go down to destruction because of man's pollution of the soil by over-farming, tearing down the windbreaks until he saw his farmland, aided by the drought, go across the skies.

I don't *feel* all that dedicated. I just feel like the normal guy. Too many people insist upon my being a legend, but I feel humble and always on the threshold of knowing how to do my work—and I love to sit and listen to music, and drink scotch.

Susan
Sontag

Susan Sontag was born in 1933 in New York City. *"The Benefactor,"* her first novel, was published in 1963. In 1965, *Against Interpretation,* a collection of her critical writings, was nominated for a National Book Award in the field of Arts and Letters. *Death Kit,* her second novel, appeared in 1967. In 1969, Farrar, Straus and Giroux published *Styles of Radical Will,* eight long essays on contemporary art and thought, and *Trip to Hanoi,* a Noonday paperback. Sontag has written and directed three films: *Duet for Cannibals* (1969) and *Brother Carl* (1971) in Sweden and *Promised Lands* (1974) in Israel. Farrar, Straus and Giroux has published screenplays of the first two films: *Duet for Cannibals* in 1970 and *Brother Carl* in 1974. Her stories have appeared in *American Review, Partisan Review, Harper's, The Atlantic, Playboy* and *Harper's Bazaar.* Her essays and reviews have been printed in numerous magazines, including *The New York Review of Books, The New Yorker, Partisan Review, Salmagundi, Tri-Quarterly, Evergreen Review, Commentary, Sight & Sound, The Nation, Vogue, Film Quarterly, Ramparts* and *The New York Times.* In 1977, Farrar, Straus and Giroux will publish *On Photography,* a series of six essays that originally appeared in *The New York Review of Books,* and a volume edited, with introductory essay and notes, by Sontag, called *Antonin Artaud: Selected Writings.* She is presently working on a third novel.

I am a writer and a filmmaker. I don't consider myself a critic, and I am above all not a critic of photography. But it's from that strictly independent and freelance position that I am saying my say; it's not as a member of the photography establishment or photography anti-establishment, but as an educated outsider.

It has occurred to me, however, that because of my special status in relation to the other people whom you have invited to talk before me that I might be in a better position than some of them to comment on the subject of this series. Obviously, to say "Photography within the Humanities" is to name two things which raise a whole series of problems. The question is: What is photography? Then there is the other big word with the little ones in between—Humanities, which makes us think of a very particular set of values that refers back to certain cultural and educational ideas, so that Humanities is a term that comes up in, above all, university curricula. But that is a kind of condensation or synthesis or anthology of the most valuable cultural experiences and ideas and works of the imagination or creation within, I say, *a* given culture. But just to catch up with it in its relatively modern form, it does have to do with a notion of curriculum.

Now if anyone would think to suggest as a title for a series of experiences or lectures or discussions, *Photography within the Humanities,* he's probably not mainly thinking of the humanities as being the subject under question but photography, because one of the first things to say about photography is that it is a relatively recent activity. Whether you consider it an art form or not, it is an activity over which people have debated (and) whose status has been under question. A lot of people in the early decades of photography tried to treat it as if it were simply some kind of copying machine, as an aid in reproducing or dispensing a certain kind of visual information, but not itself as an independent source of seeing or of material that would fundamentally change our visual sensibility, as, in fact, it has. And the history of taste and argument about photography has roughly consisted, to speak in broad terms, of the continuous upgrading of this activity.

One continues to have a great many debates, needless to say: "Is photography an art or isn't it?" This very nourishing, if phony, debate has been going on for a century about whether photography is an art or not. I say it's phony not because there are not some real questions, but because I think that the questions—at that level—are oversimplified and fundamentally opaque. But it has been, if it is a form of mystification, an immensely creative mystification. The literature about photography by professional photographers is incredibly defensive. It is both aggressive and defensive, two stances that usually go together. One can sense, under all these exalted claims that are being made for photography, a very interesting and fruitful pressure on the photographer which has been this problematic status of the very activity itself.

By asking about the situation of photography within the humanities, one is covertly raising that old query: Is photography an art?—is it really a serious activity or a serious art; does it really have a proper place in the university curriculum, as a department in museums; is it different from the other art forms? In another sense, it is as

I suggested before, a phony debate, because there is no doubt the battle has been won.

The question is rather, if photography is an art and is socially or sociologically accepted, is it an art like any other? It isn't exactly an art, like painting, and perhaps that may explain something about its current influence. In some way I would suggest that photography is not so much an art as a meta-art. It's an art which devours other art. It is a creation, a creation in the form of some certain kind of visual image, but it also cannibalizes and very concretely reproduces other forms of art; there is a creation of images, images which would not exist if we did not have the camera. But there is also a sense in which photography takes the whole world as its subject, cannibalizes all art forms, and converts them into images. And in that sense it seems a peculiarly modern art. It may be the art that is most appropriate to the fundamental terms and concerns of an industrial consumer society. It has the capacity to turn every experience, every event, every reality into a commodity or an object or image. One of the fundamental axes of modern thought is this contrast between image and reality. It doesn't seem wrong to say that our society is rooted or centered in a certain proliferation of images in a way that no other society has been.

To return to the point of departure, if photography has a place within the humanities, it might very well have a kind of central place, because it is not only a form of art under certain restrictions, but it also has a place where all kinds of sociological and moral and historical questions can be raised.

My purpose is not to evaluate the work of particular photographers, but rather to discuss the problems raised by the presence of photography, and these include moral issues as well as aesthetic issues. I think it's a perfectly good idea to study photography. I'm not talking about studying making photographs, but studying looking at them, and learning how to see, because the way in which you learn to see is a general education of sight, and its results can be extended to other ways of seeing. Another point should be made that there is such a thing as photographic seeing. If you think of people actually going out and looking for photographs as a kind of freelance artistic activity, what people have more and more learned to value is something they get in the camera that they don't get ordinarily, that they can see by means of the camera, and so they are changing their own way of seeing, in the very process of becoming habitual camera users. The world becomes a series of events that you transform into pictures, and those events have reality, so far as you have the pictures of them.

Most people in this society have the idea that to take a picture is to say, among other things: "this is worth photographing." And to appraise an event as valuable or interesting or beautiful is to wish to have a photograph of it. It has gotten built into our very way of perceiving things, that we have a fundamentally appropriative relationship to reality. We think that the properly flattering contact with anything is to want to photograph it. And the camera has indeed become part of our sensibility. So when Christopher Isherwood said, "I am a Camera," what he really meant was "I see. I see. I perceive. I am storing this up."

One of the reasons I don't take pictures is that there are a lot of other people taking them and that's for the moment enough for me; and I feel I already do see photographically. Perhaps I see too much photographically and don't wish to indulge this way of seeing any further. It is a very particular specialization of one's sensibility.

How did you first become involved with photography from the critical point of view?

I've always been a photograph junkie. That is, I've always been very interested in photographs—I cut them out of magazines and collect, not originals, but copies, reproductions of photographs. The only difference is that recently I decided to write about some of the ideas that I've had over the last twenty years. So I embarked on what I thought would be one essay and has turned out to be six. But I'm not, as I told the people who invited me to Wellesley, a photographer; I do not take photographs; I don't like to take photographs; I don't own a camera; and I'm not a photography critic. But my writing about photography represents the expression, and in a certain sense, the liquidation of a very long-term interest. It's precisely because I've been thinking about this for twenty years that I think I can write about it now. Somebody asked me what I thought I was going to do by writing these essays, and I said I'm going to cure myself of my addiction. That hasn't happened, however.

In your opinion, is the normal everyday photographer any more aggressive, cannibalistic toward the world around him or her than a normal, everyday prose writer?

There are an unlimited number of photographs to take, every photographer feels that. There are not an unlimited number of things to write, except in a very cerebral sense, which no writer really feels. Every writer has to reach and is constantly aware of how basically it comes from inside; it all has to be transformed in the homemade laboratory that you have got in your guts and your brain. Whereas, for the photographer, the world is really there; it is an incredible thing, it is all interesting and in fact, more interesting when seen through the camera than when seen with the naked eye or with real sight. The camera is this thing which can capture the world for you. It is not like a gun; it is not like doing people in, but it is a way of bringing something back. It enables you to transform the world, to miniaturize it. And photographs have a special status for us as icons and as magical objects that other visual images such as paintings and other forms of representational art such as literature do not have. I do not think that any other way of creating image systems has the same kind of obsessional power behind it.

Of course, the word "cannibalize" is loaded and provocative and is perhaps overly strong, but I do not consider it to be a key part of my argument. My primary point is not to speculate about what picture taking does to people, but to consider the impact of looking at photographs and having this kind of information or experience of the picture. It is the consumption of photographs rather than the taking of them which concerns me and why pictures have become a regular nutriment of our sensibility and a source of information.

I think there are moral issues that are worth talking about, and one shouldn't be afraid of them. I get kind of sad when I realize that what people seem to want is to be told whether photography is okay or not. I mean it's part of the world. Let me give you an example. I'm probably being very indiscreet, but I don't think he would mind—I had a call the other day from Richard Avedon, whom I had gotten to

Brassaï, *Rome-Naples Express*, 1955.

Clarence John Laughlin, *Sharley Brow in the Outhouse*, 1955, Wellesley College Museum.

Brassaï, *L'Amateur du livre au long des quais de la Seine*, 1931.

Berenice Abbott, *Multiple Exposure of a Swinging Ball in an Elliptical Orbit*, ca. 1958-1961.

Ché Guevara Dead, Vallegrande, Bolivia, 10 October 1967. *Colonel René Adriazola of the Bolivian Air Force touches chest of body Bolivian authorities said is that of Argentine-born Cuban guerilla Ernesto Ché Guevera, one-time top aide to Fidel Castro,* UPI, Wellesley College Museum.

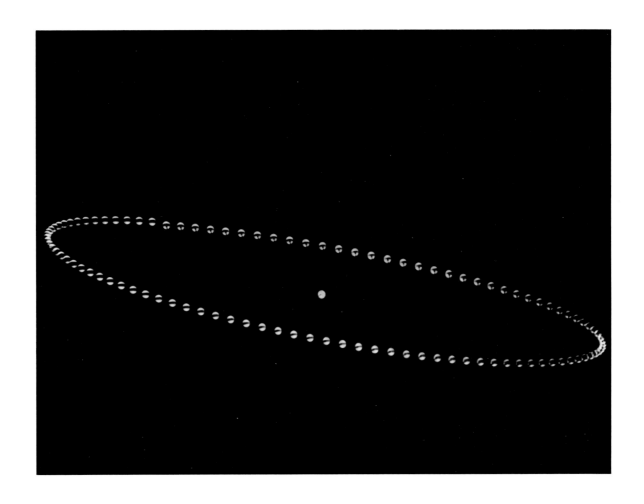

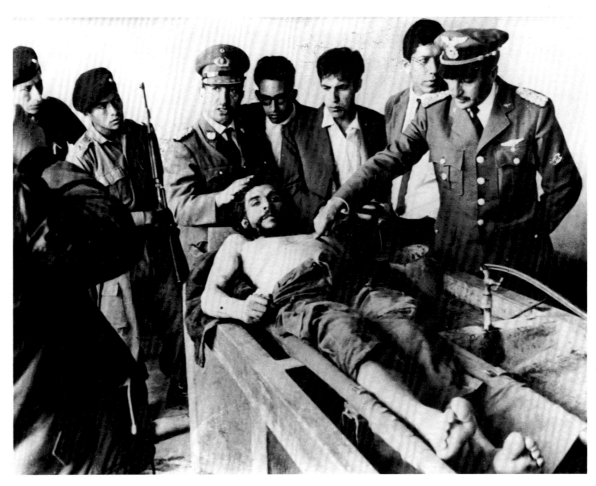

115 Susan Sontag

know as a result of these essays for the *New York Review of Books*. In fact, I didn't know him before. I don't think I would have written about photography if I had known any photographers. Anyway, we had become friends and we had a lot of discussion about the ideas of the essays, some of which he agreed with and some of which he didn't. He said, "I want to know your opinion." He had spent seven weeks in Saigon in the early seventies and he took a great many photographs of the napalm victims, victims of American bombings of the Vietnamese. He did this on his own, with his own money. He was not sent by anybody. He set up a studio in a hotel in Saigon and among other things he photographed dozens and dozens of people without faces, without hands, bodies covered with scar tissue. He was asked by a major and very commercial magazine a couple of days ago to print these photographs. He's never printed them. He's never published them. He called me up and said, "What do you think? I don't know what to do. It seems to me a terrible thing to do, and it also seems to me a good thing to do. I mean, I just don't know." We talked for an hour about it. Was it an exploitation of these people? Are these photographs aesthetic? He had only shown me one, and I haven't seen all of them. He said the photographs were beautiful. In some ways, they're beautiful and in others they are absolutely horrifying. He said, "I don't know what to do," and I said, "I don't know what you should do either; after calling me up to ask my opinion I think I'm just as puzzled as you are. I can think of very good arguments for not doing it, and I can think of very good arguments for doing it."

This is a tremendous, messy, moral problem. It doesn't start with that phone call either; it starts all the way back when one does it. If you don't publish them, you'll have some regrets; if you do publish them, you'll have some regrets. He agreed. I haven't heard the news, so I do feel a little indiscreet about telling you the story, but it's not a real secret and you may very well see these photographs in the next few weeks. But the problems are real. The complexity is real. He's very objective about his work, and he's very smart. He said they looked like Avedon pictures, and yet they are of those people. He said he was crying when he took the photographs, and yet they looked like Avedon photographs, very straight-on, white background. He said, now I don't know what to do with them. I wonder if I should have taken them, and yet I know if I had to do it all over again I would still have taken them. It's very interesting; it put his whole activity into question. I do think that people understand this. I don't think I invented these problems, and I think that a lot of photographers are aware of them. These are the real moral and aesthetic questions that are raised by this enterprise.

Do you wish that photography wasn't as ubiquitous as it is? Do you resent that kind of intrusion into your consciousness that you described as happening at age twelve when you first saw photographs of Dachau?[1]

Well, it changed my life. But I don't know that I would say I resent it. A lot of people have seen photographs that have, whether they know it or not, changed their consciousness. It's not a question of my reaction personally; it's a question of naming it—naming this phenomenon which is very formative for us . . . this shock experience . . . . It's

1. Susan Sontag, "On Photography," *New York Review of Books,* October 18, 1973.

not that I want to say that you can't be shocked by anything but a photograph, but here is this object, this image, which you can stumble or come upon inadvertently by opening the pages of a magazine. It's not like a painting; you know where the paintings are—they're in museums and galleries and if you want to go that's a special experience; you go to it, so to speak. But photographs come to you because they're all over the place.

The nature of the imagery, in which the imagery is very shocking and painful, is certainly more common now, steadily more common than it was. There was a photograph, you must have seen it, it was on the cover of both *Newsweek* and *Time* magazines a few weeks ago, of a Vietnamese mother holding a child that was wounded probably, or dying, or was already dead in her arms, facing the camera. Now this is a photograph which you would not have seen on the cover of any news magazine several years ago. I am not saying that people were not shocked by the photograph; I am sure some people cancelled their subscriptions to those magazines. But that kind of image would not have been acceptable, would have been thought too shocking by the editors of those magazines a few years ago. I think there is a process of becoming inured. I do not know if people become that much more tolerant of the real thing because the imagery becomes that much more acceptable, but inevitably there is a process of dissociation. So that often when people for the first time are confronted in reality with anything like the level of cruelty in the images they have seen, what they think is, "It's like the photograph" or "It's like the movie." They refer back to the images in order to have a direct experience of the reality because they have been prepared, in some very dissociated way, by the images and not by real experience. If you see a lot of images like that, the ante is being raised; the image has to be even more shocking to be really upsetting.

In a way you are not present, you are passive when you look at the photograph. Perhaps that is the disturbing thing. If you are standing watching an operation, next to the operating table, you can change your focus, you can still look different ways, you can change your attention—make the close-ups and the long shots for yourself. There are also the surgeons and the nurses, but you are there. You are not there in a picture, and that is where some of the anxiety comes in; there is nothing you can do when you look at a photograph.

Photographs give us information; it seems that they give us information that is very packaged and they give us the information that we are already prepared to recognize obviously. It's as if the words don't have the weight they should have, so that one of the statements being made by any photograph is: "This really exists." The photograph is a kind of job for the imagination to do something that we should have been able to do if we were not so disturbed by so many different kinds of information that are not really absorbed. Photographs have this authority of being testimony, but almost as if you have some direct contact with the thing, or as if the photograph is a piece of the thing; even though it's an image, it really is the thing.

Do you feel that photography has promoted a new kind of seeing?

Oscar Wilde said that the way you see is largely determined by art, in the larger sense. Though people have always seen, now there is a process of framing or selection which is guided by the kinds of things that we see reproduced. Photography is an art form which is basi-

Edward Weston, *MGM Studios*, 1939.

Walker Evans, *Penny Picture Display, Savannah, Georgia*, 1936.

Richard Avedon, *Jean Genet, Writer, New York City, 3-11-70*.

Lewis Hine, *Mental Institution, New Jersey*, 1924.

Duane Michals, *Portrait of Magritte*, 1965.

cally and fundamentally connected with technology and a technology whose virtues are its simplicity and its rapidity.

Cartier-Bresson has recently said that he wants to stop photographing. He has always painted a little bit, but now he wants to devote himself completely to painting, and the reason he gave is that photography promotes "fast seeing," and, having spent a lifetime seeing fast, he now wants to slow down. So he'd rather paint. The existence of the camera does promote habits of seeing which are rapid, and part of their value is how much you can get out of this rapid seeing.

Technologically, the whole history of the development of cameras has been to shorten the exposure time. Beginning a few decades ago, you got virtually instantaneous development. That means there is an increasing enlargement of the scope of the photographic project. Thus, anything can be caught by the camera, and the whole world is material to be photographed. There's no doubt that the reigning taste is for the photograph that makes the thing interesting. It isn't interesting in itself, it's interesting because it's in a photograph. One of the many tendencies is to reduce the subject matter or have a kind of throw-away subject matter in photography. There's nothing that wouldn't make a good picture. I don't think that presumption exists in the history of the other arts or—if it does—it is only recently, and partly because photography has become a model for our consciousness. When you have seen something extraordinary it goes with the telling afterwards that you want to have the photographic record of it; the notion of an event or situation or person being privileged and your taking a camera to record it are intertwined for us.

I was in China a year and a half ago and wherever I went, the Chinese said to me, "Where is your camera?" I was apparently the first person to ever come to China in the past few years (since foreigners have started going again) who hadn't gone with a camera. They understood, of course, that to get to go to China was a big thing for us foreigners and that what those foreigners did when they came to an event that was particularly interesting was to take a picture of it. I was very interested to see what people do with cameras in China, because it is the one country in the world where there is a conscious effort on the part of the Chinese leadership not to be a consumer society. Wherever I went in China, everybody had photographs of relatives: in wallets, on the glass under desks in offices, on the side of the lathe or the machine in factories. And they'd say, "That's my aunt so-and-so, or my cousin so-and-so; he lives a thousand miles away, and I haven't seen him in two years; those are my children, those are my parents." Or you'd see, less often, photographs of famous holy places or important monuments. Those are the only photographs you see. When a foreigner comes to China and takes a picture of an appealing door, the Chinese say, "What would you want to take a picture of that for?" And the person says, "Well, it's beautiful." "That door is beautiful? It needs a coat of paint." And you say, "No, it's beautiful." The Chinese do not have that idea that objects can disclose some kind of aesthetic value simply when they are reproduced, or that particularly casual, vernacular, off-hand, deteriorated, throw-away objects have a kind of poetry that a camera can reveal.

The point that I make in a number of the essays is that there is a kind of surrealist sensibility in photography which is very important, i.e., the casual ordinary thing is able to reveal its beauties when photographed. There is a whole tradition in photography, and I do not mean necessarily the so-called surrealist photographers, but precisely the people who are doing very straight-on stuff, like Weston photographing toilets and artichokes. One of the great traditions in photography is taking the neglected, homely object, the corner of something, the interesting surface, preferably a bit deteriorated or decayed with some kind of strange pattern on it. That is a way of seeing which is very much promoted by photography and has influenced people's way of seeing—whether they use cameras or not.

Is there a difference in impact between still photographs and film?

The photographs change, depending on the context in which they are seen. One could say there is something exploitative; they become items, visual commodities to be flipped through as you move on to something else. It is perhaps a way of denigrating the subject. For example, I have seen those Minamata photographs, that are downstairs, many times. I have seen them in books and all kinds of magazines, and now I am seeing them in a college art museum; each time they have looked different to me. And they are different. Photographs are these portable objects which are changed by their context. You could say, of course, that that is also true of films. To some extent, under what circumstances you see a film does change it, but the photograph is more changed by its context, especially the still photograph, because it is such a compact and portable object. This is why I tend to favor films over photographs on this question; the film establishes a proper context for the use of those images, and perhaps still photographs, in fact, are more vulnerable. I certainly think in some way a still image is and always will be more memorable. You can really remember a photograph and you can really describe it, in a way that you cannot describe two or three minutes of film.

What kinds of photographs do you find pleasing or good?

I do not know what it really means to talk about one's favorite or preferred photographs. It is funny, I learned something about my taste this afternoon that I had not seen; the people who organized this set of events asked for us to suggest ten photographs to be put in the exhibit downstairs in the museum. I sent in a list of nine photographs that meant something to me, that I had meditated about. One of the nine pictures could not be obtained, so another photograph by the same photographer was substituted. That photograph stuck out so much for me as not belonging with the others. It seemed quite clear to me that it had a different aesthetic—that anyone who had eyes could have seen that I would not have chosen that photograph, though I could have and did choose the other eight. I chose a very straight, tough, hard edged portrait photograph by Brassaï called "Rome-Naples Express." For some reason they could not get it and put this soft-focus, sentimental, touristy Brassaï photograph of a Paris bookstall on the Seine. Seeing the eight I had chosen I realized that they—in contrast with the one I had not—had something in common, even aesthetically. They all had a hard edge quality and a very high definition. All of them are upsetting, for one thing. It is funny since I have never tried to understand what makes me like one photograph over another.

Irving
Penn

Irving Penn was born in 1917, in Plain-
field, New Jersey. At art school, from
1934 to 1938, he studied design under
Alexey Brodovitch. Before turning to
the medium of photography, he ex-
plored those of drawing and painting.
Between 1937-39 his drawings appeared
in *Harper's Bazaar* and in 1942 he was
painting in Mexico. He produced his
first *Vogue* cover in 1943. His photographic work has continued to appear
in *Vogue* up to the present. Mr. Penn
has also photographed commercially
for various advertising and editorial
clients in America and abroad since
1951. He has published two books of
photographs: *Moments Preserved*
(1960), which was printed in five languages, and *Worlds in a Small Room*
(1974). Mr. Penn has exhibited in the
United States and in Europe. Prints of
his work in platinum were shown in
April, 1975, at the Galleria Civica d'Arte
Moderna, Turin, Italy, and at the
Museum of Modern Art, New York, in
May, 1975. His photographs are in the
permanent collection of several American museums, including the Museum
of Modern Art, New York and the Metropolitan Museum of Art, New York.

I see the fashion photographer in his most uncomplicated form as someone providing a useful service to industry. He is as serious in his devotion to his work and as necessary to a merchandising economy as the photographer of automobiles or the photographer of food. He is well paid, but probably no more so than he should be, given his usefulness. He is an important link in the industrial-commercial chain. His job is to record, for publication, the look of a manufactured commodity, to show its most attractive aspect and perhaps to conceal its shortcomings in the ancient skill of the marketplace.

I studied with Alexey Brodovitch. He was then art director of *Harper's Bazaar* and one of the great figures in our field. I studied design with him at art school and was invited by him to work at the *Bazaar* as an office boy during two summer vacations. I contributed drawings to *Harper's Bazaar* as my first professional work. I worked with Brodovitch as his assistant on his private assignments and then with him at a New York department store. At his suggestion I stayed on alone for one year designing the store's advertising. Then I painted in Mexico for a year. It had been my dream to paint, but after a time I began to realize that I would be only a mediocre painter. I left Mexico, returned to New York and took a job assisting *Vogue*'s new art director. I became a photographer because I came up against a blank wall in the work I was trying to do. My job was to suggest pictures for the covers of *Vogue*. I would think of ideas for the covers and visit the photographers and tell them what I wanted them to do.

Irving Penn, *Lisa Fonssagrives-Penn* (Woman in Black Dress, 1947), Copyright © 1947 by Les Editions Condé Nast, S.A.

A speech delivered at a Wellesley College photographic symposium on April 23, 1975. Published by permission of Irving Penn. Copyright © 1976 by Irving Penn.

This was unheard of in those days. Photographers simply produced pictures which they presented. They were not receptive to donated ideas—least of all from a minor member of the staff. I can understand their feelings now, but at the time, I felt that having offered the ideas and having had them rejected left me no room for continuing to work at the magazine. I discussed this with the art director, Alexander Liberman and said, "I've got to leave because I can't accomplish what you've asked me to do." He said, "Well, I can understand that. Why don't you do it yourself?" So the first color photograph I ever made became a *Vogue* cover, and it was on Liberman's urging and with his friendship and collaboration that I became a photographer and began the close relationship with him and with *Vogue* that continues to this day.

I'm really quite shocked at how time has changed the world. I don't understand much of what's going on in the women's magazines today at all, and my immediate reaction is to reject it. But then I think back to the time when I became a photographer, and I recall that people then rejected what I did as distasteful.

Irving Penn, *Black and White Vogue Cover,* Copyright © 1950 by The Condé Nast Publications Inc.

As a fashion photographer I always worked within the discipline that the girl I photographed had to be desirable, someone I'd want to put my arms around. Recently there is a new kind of girl—a girl that you might want to put your arm around out of pity, a disturbed child that you would like to soothe.

Fashion photography was very great before I came along and there were wonderful photographers. Fashion was really in Paris. The Paris panelled drawing room, which at that time was still the ideal background for the photographing of elegant women, was unknown to me. I began to photograph girls in the studio against seamless white paper. Isolating a model against a simple white background was a minor revolution. In exasperation, the magazine's editors more than once said, "Listen, you've just got to stop doing that. We're fed up with the girl alone in white space." I am surprised now that I had the courage to persist. Some years went by, and until ten or twelve years ago, there were no pictures in the magazine except girls against white paper. Now, of course, there's very little of that. One of the reasons for the change, an art director told me, is that modern clothes cannot be looked at with the same kind of eye. They cannot stand as a still life, which they were able to do in the past. So it's much better to have them taken by a photographer who uses a very small camera, who doesn't focus well and whose images are blurred and have a spirit to them. If you have the model walk along a crowded street and blur it, everything is obscured except for her spirit and vitality, which hold it all together. Because there is so little specific that's there, the viewer can project her dreams onto it. That, I think, is the secret of contemporary photography in magazines. And none of the pictures, with the exception of ones Avedon takes, can stand the examination either.

I'm not sure that I believe in the tendency today to reveal specific personal information about a model and create a duality between the private side and the mannequin side. This is a question that I understand well since I have a wife who was a great model and who faced the question all the time. As a successful model how much of your true self as a private person do you allow to get into the public print without diminishing yourself as a commodity? It's not an easy thing to decide because you're torn between your own vanity and your professionalism.

For me, who the model was as a real person was not of any significance. She was used as a symbol, and any individualism that she had, had to be obscured, because she had to be somebody with whom any reader could have identified. There had to be an anonymous quality to her, because insofar as she was being specific, she was not doing her job. A model can in one day, by jumping from taxi to taxi, and sitting to sitting, pose for a number of photographers and come out in each case a different person reflecting each photographer's projection upon her. This is close to home for me. My wife is putting together a lot of pictures, family pictures she calls them, but many of them are really professional pictures. She has posed for photographers from Man Ray and Beaton to Huene, Horst and Avedon, and it is fascinating to see that to each she is a different person. She shows me two proofs and asks me which one I prefer and I hardly recognize her in them, she was so able to change with the photographer's image of her.

The ideal of being a model, which was a very real one in the years that I began to practice fashion photography, (it was almost like being a movie star, if you were a great model) has disappeared pretty much now. Most of the important models feel that they are on their way to something else. Modeling keeps money coming in while they go to acting class, make minor movies, or follow other personal activities. As an end in itself being a model is no longer part of the American Dream.

Let me give you a typical day of a fashion sitting. At ten o'clock in the morning a bedraggled girl comes through the door, pulling a bag behind her, and she looks like the wrath of God. She's this great beauty; she's gotten there a bit late; she's unmade-up and looks terrible. And she looks kind of adorable too, because she looks like she's just awakened, and she has. She throws herself in front of a mirror and starts making faces at herself to see whether she's going to be able to pull herself together; and she turns to somebody there, some young editor, and says, "Will you please get me some breakfast?" So out goes the call for breakfast. Then she starts smearing something on her face. I come in, say good morning, and we say a few silly words, and then twenty or thirty minutes later, in comes the hairdresser. He's late too, telling how terrible everything is, he couldn't get a taxi, and so on, dragging his bag behind. This goes on and suddenly it's noon and people are beginning to think about food. Someone sends out for food, and it comes late. About one-thirty or two o'clock you get her in front of the camera. You only take three pictures, because by four o'clock the hair has gone dead, and has to be set in curlers again. People come and go with clothes, and they forget to send the earrings. It's a very time-consuming thing. The important thing from a photographer's point of view is to hold on to the image through all this debilitating, weakening nonsense.

As a man, I am pleased by a woman's paint and powder, her seductive ways of dressing, the little decorations and toys of vanity that spice her life. As a photographer I enjoy observing and studying those aspects of life and I do not apologize for my taste that sometimes leans to the frivolous and the superficial.

On the other hand, in portrait photography there is something more profound that we seek inside a person, while being painfully aware that a limitation of our medium is that the inside is recordable only insofar as it is apparent on the outside. There is a definite hour for the sitting. The subject comes to the door, we sit together for a few minutes to talk trying to find common ground, a point of sympathy and contact. During the small talk I make a commitment as to the visual direction I am going to take. I invite the subject to the camera. I begin to search for an attitude, and then begin to expose film. I follow my plan through to what may be a dead end or to success. Then we shake hands and say good-bye. Even the most sympathetic sitting never takes more than an hour and a half, small talk included. More often it's over in thirty or forty minutes.

The precarious point is where I as the photographer commit myself to the direction the picture will follow. This decision is based mostly on instinct and can turn out to have been a mistake, but I stick with it. I have found that for me it is fatal to change directions radically in the middle of a sitting. I lose the subject. His confidence goes, his eyes become glassy and I had better close the camera.

Working professionally leaves little room for failures. This is especially true in portraiture. Someone is invited to come and pose for you and you make a picture. If it's not very good it must still be published. It is embarrassing and difficult for the magazine to say, "Look, these pictures didn't come off, you better do it again." It would also be a waste of money.

But a point I'd like to make is that having to always produce a publishable result forces you to play it safer than you'd like to, because the result must be publishable. In journalism, and even more so in advertising photography, the unforgivable sin is to come out of a sitting without something that can be put on the printed page. That's worse than banality.

I began work in portraiture as a parallel activity to fashion photography. *Vogue,* the magazine I worked for, consumed an endless number of photographs of dresses and of beautiful women, but peppered through its pages were photographs of people in the arts and public life. It was the style of the publication to have these pictures be very personal and expressive (for want of a better word) where sometimes the personality of the photographer became as important as that of the subject himself. Portraiture for me was a welcome balance to the fashion diet and I was happy to go back and forth from one to the other.

Irving Penn, *Louis Jouvet, New York,
1951,* Copyright © 1960 by The Condé
Nast Publications Inc.

I invited many of the remarkable people of our time, mostly in the
arts, because that was my taste and also most useful to the magazine,
to come and pose. The invitation was usually quite loose. Since most
pictures were not being pointed to a definite publication date, we
were able to say, "when you are next in New York," or "when you
come to America."

I recall there was always a more or less noticeable difference in
mood in photographing people in the studio and in their homes. Subjects who came to the strangeness of the studio sometimes seemed to
feel themselves at a disadvantage, that their stature was not entirely
evident, that their identity had to be established before we began to
photograph. I sympathized with and understood this feeling and
tried not to confront them too soon with the apparatus of the picture
taking. There was always a time to talk, a soothing of apprehensiveness, that was a necessary prelude. I almost always did my home-
work before a sitting. I saw it as a discipline as important as checking
out the equipment. Knowing a writer's or a painter's work, or having
seen a dancer perform, is a vital ingredient in a portrait sitting. He's
sometimes overwhelmed when you know some little thing about his
professional existence. In a creative person the fabric of self-belief
can be very thin and easily damaged.

I have at times seduced myself into a mystical belief in the pene-
trative power of the camera, but reflection always brings me back to
accepting the picture process as simply the bounce back of light from
a momentary arrangement of atoms that are a face. But that is not
to say that the power of a tender word, or a clumsy one, to affect those
atoms, can be overstated. When the light and the situation for the

Irving Penn, *Picasso, Cannes, 1957,*
Copyright © 1960 by Irving Penn,
photographed on assignment for
Vogue Magazine.

portrait picture are found and the sculptural arrangement made, it
may be that the word is after all at the heart of the whole thing.

I myself have always stood in awe of the camera. I recognize it for
the instrument it is, part Stradivarius, part scalpel. I sympathize with
and respect anyone who, confronted with a portrait camera, is aware
of the consequences. Responses to the prospect of being examined by
a camera are as different as people are, but one reaction that has
been common enough for me to speak of, (and probably especially
typical of the kind of subject I have had) was that of the person in the
public eye who came to the door of the studio and seemed to be pushing ahead of him an image of himself that he wanted to have publicly
presented; and in this enterprise he wanted (and even expected!) my
collaboration. That kind of person could only be disappointed, (sometimes enraged) by the persistent penetration that portrait photography meant to me as I understood my job and my commitment.

Sensitive people faced with the prospect of a camera portrait put
on a face they think is one they would like to show the world. This
facade is protective and they are most pleased if the photographer
will idealize their fond image of themselves. I am not at all tender,
(I think of myself as neutral) as I seek to make an incision in the
presented facade. I do not think this is cruel. Very often what lies
behind the facade is rare and more wonderful than the subject knows
or dares to believe. In any event, as a journalist I have always felt
that my obligation was to the reader and not to the vanity of the
subject.

The hardest thing in the world for me is to photograph somebody
that I care about in a personal way, like a member of the family, be-

Irving Penn, *Cecil Beaton, London, 1950*, Copyright © 1958 by Les Editions Condé Nast S.A.

cause the photographic process is basically somewhat cruel. It's the kind of thing that you wouldn't want to subject someone to whom you really care about.

The idyllic existence of doing portraits for *Vogue* went on for two or three fruitful years in New York. And a couple of times each year, I was able to make trips to visit subjects in foreign countries. Portrait making on the road was similar to that in New York, although it was simpler and the equipment more portable. In New York, I depended on a large view camera, a wide bank of electric lights, and a heavy tripod. While traveling, I used the Rolleiflex, a light tripod, and the light from the nearest window. Daylight is the most delicious of the several kinds of light available to a photographer.

Over a period of years, my assignments have taken me to far places, where I have had the privilege of photographing anonymous, simple people, with most of whom I could not communicate in words. This deficiency left me unusually dependent on making use of the externals of their appearance—their costume, body paint, hair, and face make-up. The special skills and experience that came of fashion photography, being able to quickly find the essence of a costume or an attitude, were invaluable. But since these subjects were also complete people, there was always the potential of a surprise human response that could enrich the picture. In the strangeness of our relationship I could not depend on this happening, but it did happen often enough to make those results particularly worthwhile.

I wonder if the limitations I've spoken of were not sometimes more imagined than real. Because of the difference in our lives, even words in common would not have bridged the gap. In any event the lack of words threw my dependence onto physical touch. I found that a jungle person in the Pacific responded as warmly to a gentle arm around his shoulder as a nubile young girl in Africa did. And the tone of my voice, which must at times have sounded to them more like animal murmurings than intelligent speech, was everywhere understood. At times I felt a mutual understanding and human closeness with people in the savannahs of Africa or the jungles of New Guinea, that I have only rarely felt at home.

I didn't realize that a book was in the making until I was halfway through it. I was taking people out of their natural environment, putting them into studios that I had taken with me or built, and working in various parts of the world by daylight. One day I realized that there was no other place I wanted to go to continue this series: we had used up the world, and I realized that *Worlds in a Small Room* was finished. It was then important to put the individual essays together in book form, and to publish them in order to be free of the material and to be able to go on to new work.

I confess I am sensitive about this, but to tell you the truth, the book was either clobbered or generally ignored. It is still hard to find it in most bookshops. The usual criticism was, "Why was it necessary to do pictures this way? Why couldn't you have photographed your subjects where they were instead of taking them out of their own circumstances into this unnatural environment?" It is as though no one had bothered to read the text.

I'm interested in why it is not acceptable to people in book form, since it had such enormous reader interest when it came out each time in a number of *Vogue* Christmas issues. My relationship with *Vogue* through the years has been nearly an ideal one. During the most productive period my assignments were free and generous, often just, "Bring us a treasure for the next Christmas issue." That was all I really wanted to hear: usually they gave me a year to complete the assignment. It took many months of preparation; it would start with dinner with the ambassador of that country. You couldn't just barge in; it's too precarious. You might do that with a camera on your hip, but you can't deposit yourself in the middle of Africa with an entourage and a studio and say, "Look, I'm here."

One session that became part of the book may be interesting to talk about, the sitting with the Hell's Angels. I was terrified of them, physically frightened. They're terrifying, psychotic people who can kill as easily as they can love. I must tell you something that I did for self-preservation; I asked them to bring their families. So, in fact, at the time their wives and children were in the studio.

The ritual of arranging the sittings with the Angels was amusing. Our side sent an emissary, and their side sent an emissary and the emissaries talked in a preliminary meeting like foreign ministers. It was decided that we would all meet in a San Francisco park at noon. At about one minute to twelve we left our parked car. Then suddenly we heard the screech and rising pitch of their motorbikes as they came near. They parked and we approached them across the grass. They stayed where they were. We went to them.

I think they were important to me; they were visually interesting. The sitting itself was frightening. It was kind of a chancy thing to do

Irving Penn, *Andaglimb Warrior, New Guinea, 1970,* Copyright © 1974 by Irving Penn, photographed on assignment for **Vogue Magazine**.

Irving Penn, *Cuzco Children, 1948,*
Copyright © 1960 by The Condé Nast
Publications Inc.

Irving Penn, *A Young Berber Shep-
herdess, Morocco, 1971,* Copyright ©
1974 by Irving Penn, photographed on
assignment for **Vogue Magazine**.

Irving Penn, *Hell's Angel—Doug,*
Copyright © 1947 by Cowles Communi-
cations Inc.

and I wanted to see if I could pull it off. And it only half worked because I couldn't really tangle with them. I couldn't make a real picture. I could simply get an image of them and that had to do, because they were just unmanageable. In my apprehensiveness, I hurried the pictures so that the results are only half successful, although no other subjects in the book fascinate readers as the Angels do.

As a photographer, the realism of the real world is something almost unbearable to me. There's too much accidental painfulness in it. I must tell you that walking through that room downstairs and looking at the walls, I realized that there is one very old-fashioned photographer there and that's me. The photographic process for me is primarily simplification and elimination. It's that simplification that I need in a picture that really relates more to old painting and old sculpture. Dealing with the accidental accumulation of things that occurs in real life, as Walker Evans did so brilliantly, is something I can't cope with.

Photography disturbs me when it is used as propaganda, however benign. I am especially sensitive to this because it is an area of personal struggle in my work. Since I have been a commercial photographer almost all of my professional life I have come now to yearn for a personal photography that does not try to manipulate anyone.

Gene Smith's extraordinary pictures are disturbing to me not only because they show horror but also because with them, he wants to bring about certain political, social changes. To me that is a form of commercial photography. He thinks of himself as a great photojournalist; that is his genius. But for me, at least, I find his genius more in his individual images which are much finer than the units assembled as essays. I dwell on this because it's very important for photographers to face what they are trying to accomplish with their pictures.

Smith's pictures are among the most propagandistic pictures ever taken, and I'm not sure that is a very lasting quality. Consider Richard Avedon. He is brilliant in almost everything he does. But he undervalues his work done for commerce. Yet I would not be surprised if his most lasting pictures were among the things he cares least about. I feel sure that Avedon's pictures done for advertisement and as commercial fashion pages in *Harper's Bazaar* and *Vogue* are among his most brilliant photographs, and stand as one of the vital records of our lives today. You say that Robert Frank told you that he does not value his still pictures as much as his films. I am very touched by Robert Frank's pictures. Unlike Smith's, they are passive observations about society. I am pleased that he is not trying to bring about any change in me. Maybe the artist is least able to appraise what he himself does.

I'd like also to mention another area of my work, more private, and as yet unseen. Next month, May 1975, at New York's Museum of Modern Art, a group of pictures will be shown, large platinum prints of cigarettes on fine paper which I sensitize myself. I began to love what occurs when you coat good paper by hand with these remarkable metals. My delight in the material itself makes me seek out subject matter that will best take advantage of its possibilities.

My first work in platinum metals, as I was learning the medium, was in reprinting early work which had been done for the printed page, done to reach its existence in ink on a high speed press. While the platinum versions are very beautiful, they are sort of bastard

Irving Penn, *Theatre Accident,* Copyright © 1947 by The Condé Nast Publications Inc.

pictures, and I have very mixed feelings about them. They're being shown in an Italian museum at this moment, and perhaps that's where they belong. There's something somewhat uncontemporary about them. John Szarkowski, looking at these pictures said, "You know, it makes clear to me that some pictures are better in silver, some are better in platinum, but some are better in ink." He was right. These first platinum prints of mine were translations of images made for the printed page. Some vitality was sacrificed when they were beautifully printed, because they were really journalistic in their original conception.

Whereas the things to be shown in the Modern museum are completely contemporary. They may be disturbing, but they were not done for the printed page. They won't even look good on the printed page. But they are right for their medium and are meant to be seen as objects, not in ink.

What I yearn for in criticism of photography is a tactile reaction, something more visual, rather than just concepts. The contemporary critics speak around the outside of photography; they speak of it as a social document, as all kinds of things except what it is sitting there in front of us. For me, photography is nothing new. The machine is new, but photography is just the present stage of man's visual history. What I yearn for as a photographer is someone who will connect the work of photographers to that of sculptors and painters of the past. I don't think we get this from contemporary criticism.

Irving Penn, *Cigarette,* Copyright © 1974 by Irving Penn.

Robert
Coles

Robert Martin Coles was born in 1929 and educated at Harvard, Columbia, and the University of Chicago. At present, he is a research psychiatrist with the Harvard University Health Services. He has authored hundreds of articles and over fifteen books, most of which are aimed at dissolving the stereotypes that different groups of Americans hold of one another. His work has won him numerous awards and honorary degrees; the three volumes of *Children of Crisis* earned, among other distinctions, the Pulitzer Prize and the Weatherford Prize. He currently serves on the editorial board of *Aperture* and is working with a photographer in the creation of two more volumes of *Children of Crisis,* one on Indians, Chicanos, and Eskimos, the other on children of upper middle class families.

The whole issue of the relationship of writers to photographers is in certain ways a microcosm of some of the exploitative injustices that go on in this society. If I were a photographer I would be very hesitant to have the wordiness of another discipline be the means by which whatever I'm doing becomes known to, evaluated by, and responded to by other people. There is tension, I think, between the nature of our society (which is so wordy) and what the photographer is about. I don't mean to get nasty about this, bringing in St. Paul, but there is this issue of "the word," both as a source of power and of orthodoxy and ultimately of persecution, vis-à-vis "looking" and then recording, and then not saying anything, but simply going on to look once again and give life to or permanence to what is seen.

We go to museums and we watch people. They'll look at something, and they can't just look at it; they have to go and talk about it. The ultimate test is, can it be put into words? That's what I mean by exploiting the relationship. So many photographers I know will tell you that if some wordy character like myself is willing to write an introduction or a text to accompany photographs, then it can be published. Photographs themselves, except in very rare cases, do not stand on their own. I defy anyone to accept a text that would say: "LOOK, exclamation mark, signed Robert Coles." That wouldn't get very far. But if I go on and on and on and draw upon my own work and am eloquent, then they say, "The photographs are beautiful." Or, "The photographs are eloquent." I mean, how can the photographs be eloquent? Well, they're eloquent in the eyes of those who are preoccupied with words. So they use words like, "They eloquently complement Dr. Coles' moving text. At which point one is just ready to write to the critic and say, never mind!

While writers and essayists assault one another, divide themselves from one another, carry on with one another in ways that can only be called fratricidal, there is no one to pass judgment upon them with a picture: a picture of a writer at work, sitting at his desk pouring out venom, invading another field with a pen. The picture cannot do justice to what has happened between this mind and the neurophysiological system that connects with the ballpoint pen or the typewriter. But that process, if you will, can somehow come to an entire field with devastation and all too much authority, once published in an influential magazine. No one dares take issue with it, not even with the language. Photographers don't understand the complexities of that particular language. Writers don't understand it and are afraid to acknowledge that they don't understand it. And the tyranny goes on.

Why is it that so many photographers have to get involved with and be dependent on these writers? Is it the power of words, the glory of words, the editors, the publishers, the whole culture, the way we are? And what can one do to break out of that? How can the whole society break out of it, never mind me or the photographer? Write back to the publisher and say, "Listen, buddy! Cut it out! Why don't you write to Benjamin Britten and ask him to compose an opera and link it up to these photographs? And how about a sculptor?" But apparently, paper, which is what the writer and the photographer have in common, is not enough. We need words, texts, introductions to something that one looks at which seems to be quite enough sometimes, not nearly enough at other times. But believe me, not salvageable by an eloquent text.

I constantly get sent photographs of people by social activists because I'm supposed to be a social activist and because I've written some texts to photography books. I certainly don't know anything about photography that has to do with the tradition of photography. I have no right to be a critic, although it's a commentary on this field that if I wanted to become a photography critic since I write book reviews, I *could*. That shows you how awful the whole situation is. An ignorant person like me could become, if he wanted to, a photography critic. I could write a weekly column for the *New Republic* on photography books if I had the time and wanted to do it, which is a disgusting commentary. Where are the people who have some ability to evaluate photographs? Maybe those people aren't interested in writing a single word about them. This is a dilemma.

There are now very few reviews of the relatively few books on photography that have come out. So I get the feeling that there's a power problem here of some kind and that there's a clique of people that seems to control this profession. The great American tradition is supposed to have diversity and many centers of power, but I don't get that feeling about photography. For instance, Alex Harris may be the worst photographer that ever lived. He is very good—but let us speculate. Now, why should he have done one book and be working on another one just because of me? No one has really criticized or evaluated his photographs. They've evaluated the text that goes with the photographs. In each case they say, "moving, eloquent." The poor man needs a critic, but no one is giving him any help. And even if I could push him into the Museum of Modern Art, which I might be able to do from sheer arrogance and power manipulation, it's obscene how this whole thing works.

Earlier today I was discussing with some students some of the irony of my own work. I was trained in psychiatry, where even dreams have been taken over by the wordy people who insist on talking about free associations. How often do we acknowledge to ourselves, to the world at large, that a dream is not the interpretations; it's not even what is said by the patient who has the dream; but the dream is pictures? The dream is a series of pictures. There are some physiologists who say that the words come when we wake up. We don't know. How will we ever know? Who's ever going to be able to disentangle the mind? In any event, at a minimum, the dream is pictures. But you read the interpretation of dreams, you read people talking about dreams, and you get the feeling that a dream is someone who is asleep who is talking, who then wakes up and remembers what has been said, then tells it to the psychiatrist who listens, and then does yet more talking. And the whole thing is then written up, then read, then talked about and reviewed, and there are the words. *Ad infinitum,* if not, at times, *ad nauseum.*

I'm doubly tied to language. I'm a psychiatrist and so I listen to people talk (or at least I was trained to be a psychiatrist and was trained to listen to people talk, by people who, in turn, listened to me talk and made comments on what I was saying to them). When I started doing the work that I've been doing for the past twenty years I thought that I had better have a tape-recorder. And the reason I thought I needed a tape-recorder is that since I'm a scientist, if I say I have tape-recorded interviews then that will be science. If I say that I listened to someone and here is the *heart* of what I heard, or the *essence* of what I heard, or even worse, if I say I listened to someone and

I will try to *evoke* something about that person for you, then I would slip out of my authoritative, all too influential situation, and end up without even the authority that a novelist or a poet would have. So one treasures whatever credentials and authority one has come upon and purchases the nearest Sony, and goes home to a wife who is fed up with the Sony and maybe even with the methodological design of the research project. After a few weeks, one begins to think of oneself as a little confused and a little troubled and a little wacky. So then one decides to get rid of the Sony, but one can always say one has tape-recorded interviews because one *has* tape-recorded some interviews. And out in the "field" one listens and watches television and doesn't do much talking, particularly because people don't want to do much talking. Why should I talk? And what is one going to ask them? "Well, how's it going today?" "Well, it's going pretty good." "Well, how are you feeling today?" "Feeling pretty good."

This is the age of self-consciousness as we all know. Everything that we do and say has to be put into words and we have to be aware if we breathe. If we speak, if we have a thought, it's related to something else we've thought or spoken about. We have a motive, a purpose, and this must be analyzed and verbalized. We have people meeting in what's called a sensitivity group, where they talk to one another and put out on the table what's happening to them. And God forbid if anyone keeps quiet. That isn't a matter of civility, or abhorence of rudeness and vulgarity and banality; that is "resistance," and a problem. And the problem will be solved if it is spoken and if it's all out there. And of course one goes round and round, and what comes out there but all the mess that we all are? And this is a "discovery." And it is "therapeutic." One reports to a profession, to meetings, so one comes home and writes up, "This person was so-and-so and I think this and such-and-such."

Let me move from here to a story told by an Indian grandmother in New Mexico. The story is of an anthropologist who for years was collecting "data" on a reservation. He collected it, and collected it, and collected it. And she, as an informant, helped him collect it. He wrote it up and then something happened. He stopped collecting his data and started making comments. One is told by this woman that he wasn't even interested in writing his Ph.D. thesis, and that he didn't even care about all the data that he had been collecting. Whereupon one thinks, "Oh my God, a collapse." Then one is even told that he was drinking a lot. "Well, an alcoholic collapse." Then, he used to start to walk away from some of the homes out toward the mesas and look up at the sky, and sometimes take out his bottle and have a drink, and then come back. And lo and behold, as he started doing this more and more, he moved his data out of the house where he was staying and put it in his open convertible car (and this is "The Treasure of the Sierra Madre" coming up), and one day, rain, wind, thunder and lightning, and the dispersal of all this into the countryside. End of story, whereupon ever acutely one turns to her and says (because we are clinicians and we have a case history and we have to know something), "Well, *then* what happened?" And then one is told, *"That's* what happened." At which point, one thinks one needs a little bit more, how do you say it, *training*?

Again, what has all this got to do with photography? I started doing this writing and I wrote, and I wrote, and I wrote. My wife carried around a brownie camera which she liked to use with certain abandon. I started asking her if I could look at some of the pictures she'd taken of the children whom I had met and come to know. As I was trying to write about the children, somehow I felt that in those pictures there was something of a particular child that would come across to me that my mind needed to have come across, that all of the words I had written down or that I had circling around in my head were not getting at. This does not mean that there is not a value to words. This does not mean that words and pictures are antagonists. It simply means that there are times for some people when maybe a picture means something and might even change the direction of some words. Anything that will get one away from the malignant wordiness of social science is redemptive. Anything that will some-how puzzle one, and make one feel that one is inadequate to what one has seen with words, might help with words.

Alex Harris (a gifted photographer friend of mine) and I have been doing work together in New Mexico and in Alaska. It's the first time that I've really worked with a photographer and I should tell you something about how he's done his work. He must be a genius meth-odologically if not photographically. He's gone and talked to people in New Mexico who are sick and tired of anthropologists, who've been worked over by anthropologists, as you may know now, for about a hundred years. I am sure that the anthropologists must have been there even before the gold seekers were there. His "technique" is to hitchhike and be picked up by someone or to stumble into someone in a market place and talk to him. Pretty soon they're introducing him all over the place and he's taking all these pictures—the children love to have their pictures taken—and so he prints.

There is an increasing number of photographs in Alaska in the hands of the Eskimos due to his work there. Whole villages have seen themselves, in a way. And I don't mean to be facetious and sly about it: they *have* seen themselves. In a lot of these homes they don't have mirrors and they're not used to looking at themselves. They have no notion of what they look like, and could not care less, I might add. We know that to "look" is an important thing. I know myself that when these photographers come out to take my picture for magazines and so forth, it's terrible, because what I'm confronted with is my vanity, my narcissism, to use all those words, my egoism, my notion of my-self. Will this come across to the "reader," to whom I can get it to come across with *words*? With words it's under my control but once I lose that control, because the photographer has it, I feel threatened.

We all, as you know, have a notion of ourselves that has to do with mirrors and more mirrors. And I have three boys and I noticed the other day that each one has a mirror. They look at themselves in the mirror, and we teach them to look at themselves in the mirror. The point is, they have a notion of how they must appear, how they should appear, how other people look at them, how they look, and all those words having to do with looking, and being looked at, and a sense of one's self.

In our house we have these Walker Evans photographs all over, and Alex Harris photographs, and Doris Ulmann photographs. I no-ticed that my children never look at them. Maybe it's because there's just so much around for them to see: they're watching television, they have their mirrors in their rooms, there are all these things on the walls, we take them to museums. They look at one another be-

Alex Harris, *Charlie Cleveland, Shung-
nak, Alaska,* 1974.

Walker Evans, *Coal Miner's House,
Scott's Run, West Virginia,* 1936.

143 ROBERT COLES

cause they hear their mother and their father saying, "Tuck in your shirt. Your grandmother and grandfather are coming up and you have to look well." I've never heard parents in New Mexico, the rural South, or Appalachia say, "Go. Really look good because someone's coming to the house." But in these areas there's Sunday, and there's church, and there's scrubbing up, yet it is not done with quite the self-consciousness. It's done for God, whom no one sees, and it's somewhat different. This notion of what is to be seen and what is not to be seen about the self has a cultural dimension to it.

Some of the children I have come to know, like those in New Mexico and Alaska, and especially the rural children in Appalachia, have shown me what they see. Now they haven't been trained to see anything. They haven't taken any course in "visual this" or "art that" or photography. The natural landscape is part of their education. It doesn't get them any place when someone comes in and gives them a test. They are still called culturally disadvantaged by all these culturally disadvantaged people who come out of the Northeast and study them, who see very little. Actually, a lot of these characters have restricted vision, but they don't know it. I speak personally on that, not to criticize others. I have been astonished by how much more I see now than I did ten years ago. Not because I'm any smarter or better trained, but I have spent enough time with these children for them to have shown me what to look for in what they see.

Children growing up in some parts of this country may have a "self-image" as an anthropologist sees it, and that isn't the visual thing that we are connected with. It is interesting to see upper middle class and suburban children draw pictures of themselves in contrast with children from New Mexico, Alaska and Alabama. Children of the middle class have a notion of what they should be producing with the crayon or with paint and this notion is tied to what they have seen of themselves and have been taught to see of themselves as they've been growing up. It affects both what the child draws and the self-consciousness of the child if the child knows, if the child thinks to himself, "I look this way, or ought to look this way. Consequently, when I'm going to draw a picture of myself since this pain-in-the-neck character is asking me to do these things, then I've got to do it this way to evoke this reality which is part of my subjectivity." But imagine children who don't look at and who aren't taught to look at themselves. In New Mexico or Alaska, if you ask children to draw a picture of themselves, they draw a picture of a mesa, or a canyon, or a tree, or the sky, and then you keep on waiting: "Where is *you*? Draw a picture of *yourself*." And finally you get a little thing, a smear, and think, "Oh my God, is this a self-image? Is it reproducible in a book? What are they going to say in Atlantic-Little, Brown?" Particularly in the case of Alaska, where the drawings are all white and where the only thing the children are interested in is a little chalk, which I finally came up with in a moment of revelation, or white crayon, which has never been used before and can finally be used now. White crayon never even used by white people, but now used by Eskimo people, of course, because if you insist on bugging them with these drawings, they'll try and draw you something about the world. And if you want them in it you might get a line here or even a circle in white, a face. If you want to get academic and also romantic about it and make comparisons, many of the children of New Mexico and Alaska actually draw and paint as if they were Chinese or Japanese artists with a notion of nature that is much more important than any notion they have of themselves. Now, does that mean that they don't have any sense of themselves? Does that mean that there's something deficient? Or does it mean that they simply are neither really interested in, nor have been brought up to evoke themselves in, a visual way? Their use of their eyes has to do with the landscape and has to do with the outside world; it's not an inner thing. Consequently, they are having an extraordinary experience with this young photographer, Alex Harris, who's handing out these prints out there in these obscure villages. And they're looking at these perhaps the way we first looked at a television or a movie screen. Eskimo children certainly know about the movies. The movies and what television there is (which is not in the villages, but certainly is in the cities), is for them part of the language. But it's outside themselves to have this immediate experience with one's self through a photograph or with one's family through a photograph. It's a relatively rare thing. In some homes the men who went into the Army brought back from military service little twenty-five cent pictures which were regarded by some Eskimo families as we would regard the acquisition of a signed Picasso print: a very special thing to put in a special place in the house.

I found those pictures Doris Ulmann took in the South helpful to look at when I was writing about some of the children I got to know. Somehow a little picture was what you call a "methodological aid" (all those words that the social scientists use to obscure everything!). So I have been interested to hear lately that Doris Ulmann is called a pictorialist. Beware of all these people that have names! Someone wrote about her and talked about her romanticization. I thought it was an outrage because, you see, this is another problem. She, after all, went and took great pains at a particular moment when it wasn't as fashionable as it is now, went down to South Carolina and Appalachia and took these strange, haunting pictures. Now someone says she "romanticizes." Well, against what criteria? Has this person ever been in this area? Does he know what these people look like? How can a man writing in New York say, "pictorialism, romanticization," while someone else looks at it and says, "This is exactly what this is like; this isn't romantic at all, and there's nothing "pictorial" about it. It's factual, not pictorial."?

You know, I don't mean to be harsh against necessary words like "pictorialism," although it does bother me when I hear "romanticization," because that means there's a distortion of reality or a denial of an aspect of human existence. Well, maybe we have our own prejudices that are not only cultural, but have a visual quality to them. We have a notion in our minds of what a rural, Southern, black, sharecropper tenant farmer looks like. The sources of our visual prejudices would be interesting to document.

I remember once going into a migrant farmer's shack in Florida, in a town called Belle Glade. Now there are about 100,000 migrants in this area. Belle Glade somehow intrigued me, so I wandered around there for a great number of days, and eventually weeks. And I came to a cabin, where it seemed the people were the most down and out. I just thought, "This is the end of the world, this cabin. It's the end of America, it's the end of everything." And no matter how brutal a photographer could be, I would always say reality is more brutal.

Doris Ulmann, *Cleaver Meaders and Two of His Children, near Cleveland, Georgia.*

Doris Ulmann, *Ella Webster, Texana, near Murphy, North Carolina, circa 1933.*

And yet, knowing these people, one afternoon I came in and the mother was standing there with one hand on her daughter's back, and with the other hand she had some water that she had gone outside to get (they have no running water). She was pouring it on a plant, the one plant in that house. She had a plant in that house. A lovely little plant and she was watering that plant, and suddenly, I've never seen anything like this before, here was beauty that was being nourished. Now I'm not just saying it to make it sound like a good little story. The fact is, I hadn't even noticed that plant, because I didn't want to see *that*. All I was documenting was the misery and degradation of these lives. So the point is that I had not seen something that was right before my eyes. Talk about distortions! I could have told you so many other things about that family, about the way they lived, and about the work they had done. I had actually gone out in the field and worked with them, cutting celery, breaking my blasted back, doing all that kind of minute documentary reportage, and I had missed that. Now there was a softness to that moment that came across in her body, and the light was there, and the plant was there to get the sun. It was so different from those same people standing in front of that cabin looking like the end of America. So it isn't just a matter of style, I think. It's a matter of different moments in the same lives and whether the particular person, be he a writer or a photographer, *wants* to respond to it.

I have the feeling that after the photographer has come to know the people, the situation ultimately becomes an extension of what his own purposes are. If he wants to emphasize or has emphasized for himself one part of that tradition, he will find it in reality and capture it. If he's looking for another side he will find that and capture it, which is sort of like what I do. I mean, if I'm looking for trouble and want to emphasize trouble, then I'll find it. If I'm looking for strengths, I'll find them too, although I wasn't prepared maybe, by my prejudices to find them. This attitude is also interesting and relates to the whole academic tradition and what it teaches us to want to see. Particularly with the social sciences and all this talk about cultural disadvantage and cultural deprivation, we are systematically educated to find missing in people certain things, to the point that we don't see them when they're there.

I have an intense dislike for Diane Arbus. I don't like her photographs and I don't like the cult that's been made of them. Maybe it's because I'm a psychiatrist, because some part of me feels that that's wrong, that that isn't the whole of the reality. Or maybe it is that I don't want that reality evoked in photographs. But I just know that you could go into a mental hospital and you wouldn't have to come out with what Diane Arbus sees. That's, I guess, what I'm trying to say. I just know from my own experience in hospitals that it isn't only like that; people are not *only* like that. This is, in a sense, a caricature of what those people are like.

I'll tell you what the difference is between Eugene Smith and Arbus. For instance, take the dwarfs and that striking, horrible photograph of the mother and the child in the bath. Nothing could be more grotesque or horrible, but Smith is not romanticizing that, he isn't making it beautiful. When I look at his photographs, I feel the horror, but also the humanity, to use that cliché, in all its wickedness and grandeur (and I use these words advisedly) in all people: rich or poor, dwarfed, mercury-poisoned, elegant, intellectual, whatever.

Diane Arbus, *Christmas Tree in a Living Room in Levittown, Long Island,* 1963. The Museum of Modern Art.

Diane Arbus, *Woman with a Veil on Fifth Avenue, New York City,* 1968. The Museum of Modern Art.

Diane Arbus, *A Young Brooklyn Family Going for a Sunday Outing, New York City*, 1966.

And if that's brought out of me, I don't think I'm being used. It's bringing out the part of me that isn't the animal, that thinks and worries and is concerned, even though there is an animal-like side in me and in all of us. But there is a side that goes beyond self-centeredness, that goes out and reaches out to people, feels for people, and is the only hope for the survival of this world. And that's what Smith is worried about, the survival of this world and its value. And Arbus is saying, I guess, "Look at it, this is awful!" It *is* awful, but it isn't *only* awful, and I think Smith never lets you forget. And I know "hopeful" can be banal, and "hopeful" can be cheap optimism of the American phony kind, but there's some lovely tender side that he finds that is missing in Arbus.

A couple of years ago, I was asked by an American magazine to do a profile of Walker Evans. I could never bring myself to do it. I did read Hilton Kramer in the *Sunday Times*[1] and he said that Walker Evans isn't appreciated by a lot of people. He said that we see the man who went to Alabama and South Boston and took photographs, but that a lot of us don't understand the aesthetics and the surfaces of the photographs. Well, maybe we don't. I resent the duality there. I think he has in those photographs all of Oscar Handlin and Steven Phernstrom, and all of the social psychologists, who go running around doing studies, and all of *Children of Crisis,* and on and on. There's something in those homes that he has captured. And it isn't just a matter of those aesthetic words, and those academic words. Of course, there's technical expertise, and an interest in surfaces and

1. *The New York Times*, December 1, 1974.

Walker Evans, *Sharecropper's Family,
Hale County, Alabama,* 1936.

arrangements. But there is also something else that's *connecting* in
some way, even if it wasn't his personal inclination to be emotionally
connected. He connects a viewer with those people in a non-exploit-
ative way. The interest in and the response to part of the world does
come across.

But I hope I'm not a narrow-minded Marxist critic who feels that
the only beauty is proletarian beauty. The subjects of Irving Penn's
photographs are human beings who are entitled to documentation.
There's a grandeur there, but there is also a class issue of some kind.
A certain kind of person with a different view of what the world is like
might say that they are the ultimate expression of the bourgeoisie
and that Penn is documenting their arrogance, parochialism, beauty,
self-importance and their poseur quality.

How can Penn talk about Eugene Smith's work as propaganda?
This word "propaganda." I mean, my God, here is a man who gives
you a few words and he tells you what he's trying to do, presumably
in the artistic tradition. He's driven apparently to say what he's interested in doing. In that sense, I suppose all art is propaganda. But you
see how these words get thrown around: one man's propaganda is
obviously another man's beautiful vision. And what can we do? You
know, we're not in the field of chemistry or physics so there's nothing
that can be proved here.

I would like to talk about *The Old Ones in New Mexico.*[2] People
say, "Well, you know, the way you write about the way people themselves talk is not like the pictures." Why do people have to look the
way they talk? Maybe the way people look is one thing about them
and the way they talk is quite another. Maybe in some cases, the way
they look is their moment of reserve and truth, and the way they talk
is their moment of fear and panic as they come to terms with you.
And maybe a writer will eventually say, "I'm sick and tired of even

2. Robert Coles, *The Old Ones in New Mexico.* Albuquerque: University of New
   Mexico Press, December 1973.

pretending to say that what I'm writing are the tape-recorded words." But I am now getting unashamedly into what Flannery O'Connor would call 'mystery and manners.' Mystery and manners is a good way to describe a half-decent social science which is yet to be born. And all I can do with these words I write is to pray that somehow, something coming out of me will have to do with the people I write about.

A writer's obligation at this point is to shut up with the word "I" and maybe try to devise a way of describing what he has heard and seen in a way that is not the traditional first person narrative, not to mention the expository social science style. Now I don't know how you do that, although I'm trying to find that out, and I think it comes across in *The Old Ones in New Mexico*. First of all, if you want a sort of analysis of the difference, one by definition is compelled to have many much smaller statements from the people, because they are, indeed, a relatively silent people, or a terse people, or a laconic people. But what about people who are not interested in talking under any circumstances? Not because you are there, by the way, and bothering them, but because the silence is part of their being. Not total silence. Moments of conversation, moments of talk. But a different pace, a

Walker Evans, *Fireplace, Tenant Farmhouse, Hale County, Alabama,* 1936.

different rhythm, a different something. So you have to do that in the way the words come across on a page. Not quotes, but maybe you can write as if coming out of them as part of their thinking. If you can somehow deliver on the page that something inside them, fine.

For example, one meets a woman, Mrs. Lopez, by name. She tells you how she bakes. You pretend to be interested in baking. You've never been interested in baking before, although your wife has been baking all these years as has your mother before her. Who wants to be interested in baking? You can buy a loaf of bread. Mrs. Lopez is the greatest bread-maker in northern New Mexico. Certainly in the town of Touchas. Okay. A phony, dishonest ingratiating effort to get to know this woman? Eventually, in the midst of baking bread one hears a story about her children. A photographer has taken some pictures of her. She's standing there and looks—some people think she looks old and tired, some people think there's dignity to her, some people think that she's extraordinary. She tells me a story about two people, her two sons, and how she came to know that they had died, in war, one of them, and then another. One hears that story and can't forget it, goes back to it, writes about it. A photographer has spent time with her and has pictures, *another* Mrs. Lopez. And there we are.

I don't think I have in my mind that words and photographs are "the thing" itself. There is no such thing as "*the* thing" itself; it is an abstraction that you and I use. I do not speak of photography as anything closer to some ultimate reality than some words. I say that photography is another way of being.

Suggested Readings

John Morris

Articles:

BARRELL, SARAH WEBB. "The Picture Picker." *Camera 35,* February/March 1975.

FONDILLER, HARVEY V. "Magnum: Image and Reality." *35mm Photography,* Winter 1976.

JURY, MARK. "A Talk with John Morris." *New York Photographer,* June/July 1972.

MORRIS, JOHN G. "Photographers Ran the War." *Popular Photography,* February 1946.

—. "People Are People the World Over." *Ladies' Home Journal,* April 1948-March 1949. (12 articles)

—. "Confessions of a Picture Editor." New York: *Photo Notes,* Spring 1950.

—. "Let's Make Honest Pictures." *Modern Photography,* June 1950.

—. "An Appreciation: Robert Capa, Werner Bischof." New York: *Infinity,* May 1954.

—. "Magnum Photos—An International Cooperative." New York: *U.S. Camera 1954.*

—. "Chim . . . was Chim." London: *Photography,* January 1957.

—. "The World of David Seymour." New York: *Infinity,* Winter 1957.

—. "Elliott Erwitt." Lucerne: *Camera,* March 1958.

—. "Photographers Don't Think!" *Popular Photography,* December 1962.

—. "The New Look in Newspapers." *National Press Photographer,* June 1966.

—. "Where is the Money in Photography?" *Popular Photography,* October 1966.

—. "The Art of Seeing: A Guide to Travel Photography." *Holiday,* March 1968.

—. "This We Remember." *Harper's Magazine,* September 1972.

—. "How Not to Sell Your Pictures." *Popular Photography,* January 1974.

—, and Mary Adele Morris. "Your America." *Ladies' Home Journal,* June 1948.

"JOHN MORRIS' Changing *Times."* *Editor & Publisher,* 13 June 1970.

Paul Taylor

Books:

CONRAD, MAISIE and RICHARD. *Executive Order 9066: The Internment of 110,000 Japanese-Americans.* Cambridge, Massachusetts: MIT Press for the California Historical Society, 1972.

LANGE, DOROTHEA. *First Rural Rehabilitation Colonists, Northern Minnesota to Matanuska Valley, Alaska, Sailed from San Francisco, May 1, 1935.* San Francisco, 1935.

—. *Dorothea Lange Looks at the American Country Woman: A Photographic Essay by Dorothea Lange.* Fort Worth: Amon Carter Museum, 1967. With a commentary by Beaumont Newhall.

—. *The Making of a Documentary Photographer.* mimeographed, Berkeley: University of California, Bancroft Library, Regional History Office, 1968. An interview conducted by Suzanne Riess.

—, and Margaretta Mitchell. *To a Cabin.* New York: Grossman Publishers, 1973.

—, and Paul Schuster Taylor. *An American Exodus: A Record of Human Erosion.* New York: Reynal and Hitchcock, 1939.

—. *An American Exodus: A Record of Human Erosion.* Revised and extended edition. New Haven: Yale University Press, 1969.

MUSEUM OF MODERN ART, New York. *Dorothea Lange.* New York: Doubleday, 1968. Introductory essay by George P. Elliott.

STRYKER, ROY EMERSON, and NANCY WOOD. *In This Proud Land: America 1935-1943 As Seen in the FSA Photographs.* Greenwich, Connecticut: New York Graphic Society Ltd., 1973.

TAYLOR, PAUL SCHUSTER. *Paul Schuster Taylor, California Social Scientist.* mimeographed, Berkeley: University of California, Bancroft Library, Regional History Office, 1973. An interview conducted by Suzanne Riess.

Gjon Mili

Books:

MILI, GJON. *The Magic of the Opera.* New York: F. H. Praeger, Inc., 1960.

—. *Picasso's Third Dimension.* Friton Press, 1970.

Articles:

—. "Gjon Mili Photographs Ballet Dancers at High Speed." *Life,* 19 February 1940.

—. "World Charter." *Life,* 23 July 1945. Day-by-day coverage of the United Nations at the San Francisco conference.

—. "The World of Sean O'Casey." *Life,* 26 July 1954.

—. "Queen of Cathedrals." *Life,* 15 December 1961. An expressionist essay on Chartres.

—. "The Relentless Spectre of Brecht." *Life,* 18 September 1964.

—. "Mr. B. Talks about Ballet." *Life,* 11 June 1965.

—. "Serenade to Ninety Years of Greatness." *Life,* 11 November 1966.

—. "An American Masterpiece." *Life,* 3 October 1969. A translation into photographs of Jerome Robbins' ballet, "Dancers at a Gathering."

Films:

—. *Jamming the Blues,* 1944.

—. *Raoul Dufy Paints, New York,* 1950 (10 min.)

—. *Casals, Prades Festival,* 1950 (15 min.)

—. *Jean Babilée, Dancer,* 1951 (4 min.)

—. *Salvator Dali,* 1951 (6 min.)

—. *Stomping for Mili, Brubeck Jazz Quartet,* 1955 (10 min.)

—. *Eisenstadt Photographs "The Tall Man,"* 1955 (15 min.)

—. *"Tempest," filmmaking on location,* 1958 (15 min.)

—. *Henri Cartier-Bresson, Photographer,* 1958 (3 min.)

—. *Hommage to Picasso,* 1967 (6 min.)

Robert Frank

Books:

BISCHOF, WERNER, ROBERT FRANK, and PIERRE VERGER. *Indiens pas morts.* Text by Georges Arnaud. Paris: Editions Robert Delpire, 1956. English edition: *Incas to Indians.*

FRANK, ROBERT. *Les Américains.* Edited by Robert Delpire. Paris, 1958.

—. *The Americans.* American edition. New York: Aperture, Inc., Grossman Publishers, 1959, 1969. With an introduction by Jack Kerouac.

—. *Pull My Daisy.* Text by Jack Kerouac. New York: Grove Press, Inc., 1961.

—. *The Lines of My Hand.* Los Angeles: Lustrum Press, 1972. Japanese edition: Tokyo: Kazuhiko Motomura, 1971.

GREEN, JONATHAN, ed. *The Snapshot. Aperture,* vol. 19, no. 1. New York: Aperture, Inc., 1974.

Articles:

BENNETT, E. "Black and White are the Colors of Robert Frank." *Aperture,* vol. 9, no. 1, 1961, pp. 20-22.

DESCHIN, J. "Coney Island." *Camera,* 50, 1971, pp. 19-25.

FRANK, ROBERT. "The Congressional." *Fortune,* November 1955, pp. 118-122. With text by Walker Evans.

—. "Photographs." *Aperture,* vol. 9, no. 1, 1961, pp. 4-19.

—. "Bus Ride Through New York: the Bridge from Photography to Cinematography." *Camera,* 45, 1966, pp. 32-35.

—. "Films: Entertainment Shacked up with Art." *Arts* 41, 1967, p. 23.

—. "Photographs of Women." *Camera,* 51, 1972, p. 32.

GIBSON, RALPH. "Review of *The Americans.*" *Artforum* 8, 1970, p. 92.

"John Simon Guggenheim Memorial Foundation Fellows in Photography 1937-1965." *Camera,* 45, 1966, p. 5.

Still/3. "Dialogue between Robert Frank and Walker Evans." New Haven: Yale University Press, 1973.

STOTT, W., "Walker Evans, Robert Frank and the Landscape of Dissociation." *ArtsCanada,* 31, 1974, pp. 83-89.

"The Street." *Camera,* 48, 1969, pp. 6-13.

Films:

—. *Pull My Daisy,* 1959-60.

—. *The Sin of Jesus,* 1961.

—. *OK End Here,* 1963.

—. *Me and My Brother,* 1965-68.

—. *Conversations in Vermont,* 1969.

—. *Life Raft Earth,* 1970.

—. *About Me—A Musical about my Life in New York,* 1971.

Frederick Wiseman

Books:

—. "An Interview with Frederick Wiseman." in Levin, G. Roy. *Documentary Explorations: 15 Interviews with Film-Makers.* Garden City: Anchor Press, Doubleday & Co., Inc., 1971.

—. "An Interview with Frederick Wiseman." in Rosenthal, Alan. *The New Documentary in Action: A Casebook in Film Making.* Berkeley and Los Angeles: University of California Press, 1972.

Articles:

GRAHAM, JOHN. " 'There Are No Simple Solutions': Frederick Wiseman on Viewing Film." *Film Journal,* Spring 1971, pp. 44-47. An interview.

HANDLEMAN, JANET. "An Interview with Frederick Wiseman." *Film Library Quarterly,* Summer 1970, pp. 5-9.

MAMBER, STEPHEN, "The New Documentaries of Frederick Wiseman." *Cinema,* 6, no. 1, pp. 33-40.

McWILLIAMS, DONALD E. "Frederick Wiseman." *Film Quarterly,* Fall 1970, pp. 17-26.

SULLIVAN, PATRICK J. " 'What's All the Cryin' About?' The Films of Frederick Wiseman." *Massachusetts Review,* Summer 1972, pp. 452-468.

Films:

—. *Titicut Follies,* 1967.

—. *High School,* 1968.

—. *Law and Order,* 1969.

—. *Hospital,* 1970.

—. *Basic Training,* 1971.

—. *Essene,* 1972.

—. *Juvenile Court,* 1973.

—. *Primate,* 1974.

—. *Welfare,* 1975.

—. *Meat,* 1976.

John Szarkowski

Books:

FRIEDLANDER, LEE and JOHN SZARKOWSKI. *E. J. Bellocq: Storyville Portraits.* New York: The Museum of Modern Art, 1970.

HOLMES, SAM and JOHN SZARKOWSKI. *Photographs and Anti-Photographs: Elliott Erwitt.* Greenwich, Connecticut: New York Graphic Society, 1972.

SZARKOWSKI, JOHN. *The Idea of Louis Sullivan.* Minneapolis: University of Minnesota Press, 1956.

—. *The Face of Minnesota.* Minneapolis: University of Minnesota Press, 1958.

—. *The Photographer and the American Landscape.* New York: The Museum of Modern Art, 1963.

—. *The Photographs of Jacques Henri Lartigue.* New York: The Museum of Modern Art, 1963.

—. *André Kertész: Photographer.* New York: The Museum of Modern Art, 1964.

—. *The Photographer's Eye.* New York: The Museum of Modern Art, 1966.

—. *Walker Evans.* New York: The Museum of Modern Art, 1971.

—. *From the Picture Press.* New York: The Museum of Modern Art, 1973.

—. *Looking at Photographs: 100 Pictures from the Collection of The Museum of Modern Art.* New York: The Museum of Modern Art, 1973.

—. "Atget's Trees." in *One Hundred Years of Photographic History: Essays in Honor of Beaumont Newhall.* Edited by Van Deren Coke. Albuquerque: University of New Mexico Press, 1975.

—, and Shoji Yamagishi, eds. *New Japanese Photography.* New York: The Museum of Modern Art, 1974.

WINOGRAND, GARRY. *The Animals.* Afterward by John Szarkowski. New York: The Museum of Modern Art, 1969.

Articles:

SZARKOWSKI, JOHN. "Photographing Architecture." *Art in America,* no. 2, 1959, pp. 84-90.

—. "Photography and the Mass Media." *Aperture* 13, 1967, pp. 182-184.

—. "A Different Kind of Art." *New York Times Magazine,* 13 April 1975.

Eugene Smith

Books:

HICKS, WILSON. *Words and Pictures.* Arno Press, 1973.

SMITH, W. EUGENE, and AILEEN M. *Minamata.* New York: Holt, Rinehart and Winston, 1975.

W. EUGENE SMITH: *Photographs and Notes.* An Aperture Monograph. New York: Aperture, Inc., 1969.

Articles:

SMITH, W. EUGENE. "Country Doctor." *Life,* 20 September 1948, pp. 115-126.

—. "Spanish Village." *Life,* 9 April 1951, pp. 120-129.

—. "Nurse Midwife." *Life,* 3 December 1951, pp. 134-145.

—. "A Man of Mercy." *Life,* 15 November 1954, pp. 161-172.

Susan Sontag

Books:

SONTAG, SUSAN. *Against Interpretation.* New York: Delta Books, Dell Publishing Company, 1966.

—. *Death Kit.* New York: Farrar, Straus and Giroux, 1967.

—. *Styles of Radical Will.* New York: Farrar, Straus and Giroux, 1969.

—. *Duet for Cannibals.* New York: Viking Press, 1970.

—. *Brother Carl.* New York: Farrar, Straus and Giroux, 1974.

—. *On Photography.* New York: Farrar, Straus and Giroux, forthcoming.

Articles:

—. "On Photography." *New York Review of Books,* 18 October 1973, p. 59.

—. "Freak Show." *New York Review of Books,* 15 November 1973. p. 13.

—. "Shooting America." *New York Review of Books,* 18 April 1974, p. 17.

—. "Photography: the Beauty Treatment." *New York Review of Books,* 28 November 1974, p. 35.

—. "Fascinating Fascism." *New York Review of Books,* 6 February 1975, p. 23.

—. "Photography in Search of Itself." *New York Review of Books,* 20 January 1977, p. 53.

Films:

—. *Duett för kannibaler (Duet for Cannibals,* 1969).

—. *Brother Carl,* 1971.

—. *Promised Lands,* 1974.

Irving Penn

Books:

PENN, IRVING. *Moments Preserved.* New York: Simon and Schuster, 1960.

—. *Worlds in a Small Room.* New York: Grossman Publishers, 1974.

Photographs:

Vogue magazine, 1943 to the present.

Robert Coles

Books:

COLES, ROBERT. *The Desegration of Southern Schools.* New York: New York Anti-Defamation League of B'nai Brith, 1963.

—. *Children of Crisis: A Study of Courage and Fear.* Boston: Atlantic-Little, Brown and Company, May 1967.

—. *Dead End School.* Boston: Atlantic-Little, Brown, April 1968.

—. *The Grass Pipe.* Boston: Atlantic-Little, Brown, April, 1969.

—. *Still Hungry in America.* Photographs by Al Clayton. World Publishing—New American Library, April 1969.

—. *The Image is You.* Edited by Donald Erceg. Boston: Houghton-Mifflin, September 1969.

—. *Wages of Neglect.* Chicago: Quadrangle Press, October 1969.

—. *Uprooted Children: The Early Lives of Migrant Farmers.* Pittsburgh: University of Pittsburgh Press, February 1970.

—. *The Middle Americans.* Photographs by Jon Erikson. Boston: Atlantic-Little, Brown, June 1970.

—. *Teachers and the Children of Poverty.* Washington: The Potomac Institute, June 1970.

—. *Drugs and Youth: Medical, Psychiatric and Legal Facts.* Liveright Publishing, June 1970.

—. *Erik H. Erikson: The Growth of His Work.* Boston: Atlantic-Little, Brown, November 1970.

—. *The Geography of Faith: Conversations between Daniel Berrigan, when Underground, and Robert Coles.* Boston: Beacon Press, October 1971.

—. *Migrants, Sharecroppers and Mountaineers.* Volume II of *Children of Crisis.* Boston: Atlantic-Little, Brown, January 1972.

—. *The South Goes North.* Volume III of *Children of Crisis.* Boston: Atlantic-Little, Brown, January 1972.

—. *Saving Face.* Boston: Atlantic-Little, Brown, March 1972.

—. *Farewell to the South.* Boston: Atlantic-Little, Brown, July 1972.

—. *A Spectacle Unto the World Catholic Worker Movement.* New York: Viking Press, June 1973.

—. *Riding Free.* Boston: Atlantic-Little, Brown, September 1973.

—. *The Old Ones of New Mexico.* Albuquerque: University of New Mexico Press, December 1973.

—. *The Darkness and the Light.* Photographs by Doris Ulmann. New York: Aperture, Inc., July 1974.

—. *The Buses Roll.* New York: W. W. Norton and Company, October 1974.

—. *Irony in the Mind's Life: Essays on Novels by James Agee, Elizabeth Bowen, and George Eliot.* Charlottesville: University of Virginia Press, 1974.

—. *Headsparks.* Boston: Atlantic-Little, Brown, April 1975.

—. *William Carlos Williams: The Knack of Survival in America.* New Brunswick, N.J.: Rutgers University Press, July 1975.

—. *The Mind's Fate.* Boston: Atlantic-Little, Brown, August 1975.

O'CONNOR, FLANNERY. *Mystery and Manners.* New York: Farrar, Straus and Giroux, 1957.

Articles:

COLES, ROBERT. "Looking and Listening." *Aperture,* Vol. 19, no. 4, 1975.

Photo Credits

Arnold Crane, pp. 5, 7 (collection E.P. Janis).

Donald Dietz, pp. 96, 122 bottom.

Larry Edwards, pp. 12, 26, 52, 66.

Stephen Frank, pp. 110, 122 top, 138.

Lyndon Baines Johnson Library, Austin, Texas, p. 23, Okamoto.

Library of Congress, Farm Security Administration files, pp. 143 bottom, 150.

Magnum Photos, Inc., New York, p. 22.

Linda Mahoney, p. 78 top.

The Museum of Modern Art, Department of Public Information, pp. 82, 83.

New York Times, p. 23, Lien.

The Oakland Museum, Art Department, Oakland, California, pp. 27, 28, 31 bottom, 32, 36, 37, 40 top left.

Time-Life Picture Agency, © Time, Inc., pp. 19, 20.

Compix UPI News Pictures, p. 115 bottom.

Wide World Photos, Inc., p. 15, Fass, Adams, Browne, Ut; p. 23, Atkins.